need to know?

Kings & Queens

Collins

First published in 2006 by Collins
an imprint of
HarperCollins Publishers
77–85 Fulham Palace Road
London W6 8JB

www.collins.co.uk

A catalogue record for this book is available from
the British Library

Senior editor: Sarah Goulding
Editor: Anna Groves
Designer: Mike Spender
Series design: Mark Thomson
Front cover photograph: Francis G. Mayer/CORBIS
Back cover photographs from top to bottom:
DIOMEDIA/Alamy
Andrew Sadler/Alamy
Dynamic Graphics Group/Creatas/Alamy
Justin Kase/Alamy
Khaled Kassem/Alamy

ISBN-13 978-0-00-721802-8
ISBN-10 0-00-721802-8

Colour reproduction by Colourscan, Singapore
Printed and bound by Printing Express Ltd,
Hong Kong

Contents

Introduction

In many early societies, long before they became organized into states governed by written laws, there existed the figure of the sacrificial king, a figure partly religious (sometimes regarded as a god or a kind of high priest), partly a symbol representing the spirit of the people, and partly a kind of good-luck token. In some societies, such individuals were actually killed at the end of their appointed reign in a ritual connected with the harvest.

These earliest kings had no power. They were neither rulers nor war leaders, but symbols and representatives. There is little connection between the sacrificial king of prehistoric times and the war-making, law-giving kings of medieval Europe, still less with the modern monarchy. Yet this aspect of monarchy, as the symbol of a nation and representative of the people, has survived during the many great changes that have taken place through the centuries. We no longer contemplate cutting a monarch's throat to encourage the crops, but it is essentially that ancient role of national symbol that the monarchy fills today.

As a result of events in the past thousand years or so we have come to regard the monarchy as a political institution: the Queen is, after all, the Head of State. But the once-great political power of the monarchy has been whittled away until practically nothing remains, while the older notion of the monarch as the symbol of national unity is probably as strong as ever it was. Because it is difficult to define, this aspect of monarchy is sometimes underrated or overlooked. It is much easier to describe the Queen's role in the constitution, or her relations with her prime ministers, or her household expenses, yet these are minor matters compared with the almost mystical sense of the monarch as the embodiment of a national idea.`

A medieval king

Modern monarchy

The role of a monarch today has little to do with politics or economics. Monarchy cannot be audited and is hard to justify in a modern, democratic society. It is undoubtedly an anachronism, but for many it does seem to fulfil a need. The British monarchy, despite its ups and downs, remains remarkably popular.

Survival

The British monarchy is not as ancient as the imperial dynasty of Japan, nor quite as old as the Papacy, but it is still one of the most venerable institutions in the world. It has survived many crises, including a brief disappearance in the seventeenth century, and its character has undergone radical change. That it has survived the past two centuries, when crowns were tumbling all around, is partly due to the qualities of recent monarchs. It may also be a decisive factor in its future survival.

An illustration from the Magna Carta

1 Scotland, Ireland and Wales

Although relatively little known due to the scarcity of historical records, the rulers of Scotland, Ireland and Wales provide a fascinating glimpse into Britain's past. Covering the Celts, the Romans and the union of the Scottish and English crowns along with the Irish kings and major Welsh rulers, some colourful characters and major historical events feature here.

Kings of Scots

The Romans

Gnaeus Julius Agricola (ad 40-93), Roman governor of Britain, invaded Caledonia (Scotland) in ad 81. He defeated the Celtic tribes under their leader, Calgacus, at the battle of Mons Graupius (ad 83), in eastern Scotland.

Saxon warrior

The difficult country and fierce resistance of the tribes convinced the Romans that Caledonia could not be conquered and held. The Roman Emperor Hadrian ordered the building of a defensive wall (122–26) between the Solway and the Tyne. A few later sorties notwithstanding, Hadrian's Wall marked the northern limit of the Roman Empire.

In the fifth century Scotland was divided between four peoples. The **Picts**, who were Celts, were the strongest, controlling the country from the Forth to Caithness. Another Celtic people inhabited **Strathclyde**, from Cumbria to the Solway. The **Scots** occupied the kingdom of Dalriada in Kintyre, Argyll and neighbouring isles. They were Celts who came from northern Ireland in about the third

Emperor Hadrian and/or fourth centuries. Their kings were to establish what became the Scottish monarchy. South-east Scotland was occupied by Anglo-Saxons, who created the kingdom of **Northumbria** in the early seventh century.

House of Fergus, or Alpin

Fergus was the semi-legendary chief of the Scots of Dalriada, said to have established the capital at Dunadd, near Crinan, c.500. His successors before the ninth century are obscure.

The succession of early Scottish kings is complicated by the custom of passing the Crown between different branches of the dynasty in succeeding generations. In an age when kings frequently died by violence and comparatively young, this custom ensured that the Crown was likely to be inherited by a mature man rather than a child.

Kenneth Mac Alpin (died 858), regarded as the founder of the monarchy in Scotland, was the son of Alpin, King of Dalriada, and a Pictish princess. He succeeded his father in 834 and, after defeating the Picts in 843, united virtually all of Scotland north of the Forth in his kingdom of Alba, or Alban.

Kenneth Mac Alpin founded the ecclesiastical capital at Dunkeld and made his secular capital at Forteviot. He had at least five children. His two sons later became kings. His three daughters married, respectively, the King of Strathclyde; the Norse King of Dublin, Olaf the White; and the High King of Ireland, Aedh Finnlaith.

Donald I (reigned 858-62), brother of Kenneth Mac Alpin, possibly died in battle (few of these Kings of Scots died peacefully) against the Norsemen.

Constantine I (reigned 862-77), son of Kenneth Mac Alpin, died in battle against the Norsemen.

Aedh (reigned 877-78), another son of Kenneth Mac Alpin, died in battle, possibly buried at Maiden Stone, Aberdeen.

Eochaid (reigned 878-89), son of Run Macarthagail, King of Strathclyde, whose wife was a daughter of Kenneth Mac Alpin. Through his father, he was also King of Strathclyde. He was deposed shortly before his death and apparently had no issue.

Donald II (reigned 889-900), only son of Constantine I. He was killed in battle and buried, like most early kings of Scots, on the holy isle of Iona.

Constantine II (reigned 900-42, died 952), son of Aedh. He acknowledged the English king Edward the Elder as overlord (see page 80), and was defeated by the English at the battle of Brunanburgh (937). He abdicated in order to become a monk at St Andrews, subsequently being elected abbot.

Scotland, Ireland and Wales

Malcolm I (reigned 942-54), son of Donald II, was killed in a battle with the men of Moray and buried at Iona.

Indulf (reigned 954-62), son of Constantine II. Like his father, he abdicated in order to enter a monastery, but shortly afterwards he was killed during a Norse raid.

Duff (reigned 962-66/7), son of Malcolm I, died in battle.

Colin (Cuilean) (reigned 966/7-71), son of Indulf, was killed in battle against the King of Strathclyde.

Kenneth II (reigned 971-95), son of Malcolm I, was murdered by supporters of his successor.

Constantine III (reigned 995-97), son of Colin, was killed, probably murdered, at Rathinveramon.

Kenneth III (reigned 997-1005), son of Duff, was killed in battle against his successor.

A Scottish king

did you know?

Scotland's monarchy originates from two sources. The Scottish-Irish side made its way from County Antrim to Scotland in 498 AD when three brothers, Loarn, Fergus and Angus MacErc, left Ireland and setted in Argyllshire, on the west coast. The east coast of Scotland was populated by the Picts, and the two families had merged by 841 AD.

Malcolm II

must know

Born: c.954
Parents: Kenneth II and a Leinster princess
Ascended the throne: 25 March 1005
Reign: 18 years
Married: Name unknown
Children: Two or three daughters, including Bethoc, the lady of Atholl
Died: Glamis, 25 November 1034

The last of the House of Alpin, it appears that Malcolm ruled only part of Scotland during his reign, in opposition to leaders from Moray such as Finlay MacRory, Mormaer of Moray and father of Macbeth. In 1006, Malcolm was defeated by Northumbrian forces at Durham. The English then became preoccupied with the Danish, allowing Malcolm to march south, avenging the loss at Durham by winning the Battle of Carham (1018), thus gaining Lothian. Thirteen years later, however, Canute, king of England, Denmark and Norway, invaded Scotland, probably because Malcolm had been making alliances with the Danes, and forced the Scottish king to submit to him (submission was a traditional expression of personal homage). However, Canute seems to have recognised Malcolm's possession of Lothian.

The marrriage of his daugher to Sigurd the Stout, Earl of Orkney, extended Malcolm's influence to the far north. He battled to expand his kingdom, gaining land down to the River Tweed in Strathclyde. When Malcolm's ally in the Battle of Carham, King Owen the Bald of Strathclyde, died without an heir, Malcolm gained Strathclyde for his grandson, Duncan. This caused dissent throughout the kingdom of Strathclyde which resulted in Malcolm's murder at Glamis in 1034. He was buried on the Isle of Iona shortly after.

The House of Dunkeld

Since Malcolm II had no male heir, the succession passed to the House of Dunkeld through the marriage of his daughter, Bethoc, to Crinan, lay Abbot of Dunkeld. The dynasty lasted until 1290. Its members were somewhat less prone than their predecessors to violent and early death.

Duncan I

> **must know**
>
> **Born:** c.1001
> **Parents:** Crinan (Cronan), Mormaer of Atholl and lay Abbot of Dunkeld,
> and Bethoc, daughter of Malcolm II
> **Ascended the throne:** November 1034
> **Reign:** Six years
> **Married:** Sybilla, daughter or sister of the Earl of Northumbria
> **Children:** Three sons, including Malcolm III and Donald III, and probably one daughter
> **Died:** 1 August 1040

Duncan's reign was short and unsuccessful. He was an incompetent ruler and, even worse, a bad military leader. He failed in all his efforts to invade Northumbria and Caithness. Having abandoned this campaign, Duncan's next target was Thorfinn, Earl of Orkney, who was Macbeth's half-brother. Macbeth came to Thorfinn's aid and, in a battle at Pitgaveny Elgin in 1040, Duncan was killed. Duncan had heirs but the oldest of his sons was only was only nine years old at the time, and the prospect of a child on the throne was unthinkable. Macbeth, however was a grown man and he was duly elected king.

Macbeth

> **must know**
>
> **Born:** c.1005
> **Parents:** Finlay MacRory, Mormaer of Moray, and Donada,
> daughter of either Kenneth II or Malcolm II
> **Ascended the throne:** 14 August 1040
> **Reign:** 17 years
> **Married:** Gruoch (Gruach), a granddaughter of Kenneth III
> **Children:** None
> **Died:** 15 August 1057

> **did you know?**
>
> The Macbeth in Shakespeare's play is portrayed as a murderous villain who would stop at nothing to get what he wanted. The real Macbeth was, in fact, a great monarch, loved and respected by his subjects. He achieved a period of relative peace in Scotland during his reign.

Macbeth (or Maelbeatha) was unfairly treated by Shakespeare, his reign being longer and his rule more capable than the English playwright suggested. Far from being the muderous thane steeped in the blood of the saintly Duncan, the real-life Macbeth was a wise, strong ruler, loved and respected by his subjects, who managed to preserve the peace of his realm for 14 years – an extraordinary achievement in such a turbulent and unruly place as medieval Scotland.

He claimed the throne through his wife and proved to be a pious, generous monarch. Proof that Macbeth was secure on his throne came in 1050, when he went on a pilgrimage to Rome. No medieval monarch would have risked leaving his kingdom if he was unsure of its security.

Meanwhile, however, young Malcolm was growing up and had never lost sight of the fact that he, and not Macbeth, was the true king of Scotland. In 1057, aided by Edward the Confessor, Malcolm and English allies led by Earl Siward of Northumbria dealt Macbeth a defeat at Dunsinane, near Scone in Perthshire. Macbeth withdrew and Malcolm pursued, catching up with him and killing him at Lumphanan near Aberdeen.

Macbeth instructing murderers to kill Banquo

Lulach

must know

Born: c.1030
Parents: Gillacomgain, Mormaer of Moray, and Gruoch, who married Macbeth as her second husband
Ascended the throne: 15 August 1057
Crowned: Scone, August 1057
Reign: Seven months
Married: A daughter of the Mormaer of Angus
Children: One son, one daughter
Died: Essier, Strathbogie, 17 March 1058

did you know?

Lulach appears to have been a weak king, and was apparently known as Lulach the Simple or Lulach the Fool. He does, however, have the distinction of being the first king of Scotland for whom there are coronation details available. He was crowned in August 1057 at Scone Abbey in Perthshire, Scotland.

Macbeth's stepson and immediate successor was the first King of Scots known to have taken part in a coronation ritual at Scone. Lulach was killed by Malcolm III less than a year after succeeding Macbeth.

Malcolm III

Malcolm III

must know

Born: c.1031
Parents: Duncan I and Sybilla of Northumbria
Ascended the throne: 17 March 1058
Reign: 35 years
Married: (1) Ingibiorg, widow of Earl Thorfinn II of Orkney, (2) Margaret, granddaughter of King Edmund II of England
Children: With (1), three sons, including the future Duncan II; with (2), seven sons, including three future kings, and two daughters
Died: Alnwick, 13 November 1093
Buried: Tynemouth

King Malcolm III

Malcolm III was brought up in England from the age of nine, and in 1069 married an English princess, later canonized as St Margaret for her patronage of the Church.

The couple introduced a strong English influence into both lay and ecclesiastical society. The centre of gravity of the kingdom moved south, into Anglo-Saxon Lothian and away from the Celtic north.

After the Norman Conquest of England, Malcolm supported the claims of Margaret's brother, Edgar the Aetheling, to the English throne and launched a series of raids into northern England. After a retaliatory invasion by William the Conqueror, Malcolm paid homage to him at Abernethy in 1071. He was ambushed and killed while besieging Alnwick on his final Northumbrian raid. Margaret died a few days later.

Donald III

must know

Born: c.1033
Parents: Duncan I and Sybilla of Northumbria
Ascended the throne: 13 November 1093
Reign: Four years
Married: Unknown
Children: One daughter, Bethoc
Died: Rescobie, Forfar, 1099
Buried: Dunkeld, later removed to Iona

did you know?

The minor character of Donalbain in Shakespeare's play *Macbeth* is loosely based on Donald III. He took the throne of Scotland in 1093 on the death of his brother Malcolm III, in a joint rule with his nephew Edmund I. No record exists to indicate that Donald was ever crowned.

Donald Ban, or Donaldbane, which in the Gaelic language means 'Fair Donald', seized the throne on the death of his brother, Malcolm III, in a joint rule with his nephew Edmund I. Donald ruled the north of the kingdom and Edmund ruled the south.

Donald's background was Celtic and Norse and he reversed Malcolm's Anglo-Norman policies. Attacked by Malcolm's sons, with English support, he lost the throne (1094), regained it, but was again deposed (1097), dying in captivity. He was the last member of the House of Dunkeld to be buried in Iona, which subsequently fell to the Norsemen.

Duncan II

must know

Born: c.1060
Parents: Malcolm III and Ingibiorg
Ascended the throne: May 1094
Reign: Six months
Married: Ethelreda, daughter of Earl Gospatrick of Northumbria
Children: One son, William
Died: 12 November 1094
Buried: Dunfermline Abbey

did you know?

For a time, Duncan II lived as a hostage in England. He became king of the Scots after driving out his uncle, Donald III, in 1093, an enterprise in which he was helped by the English and the Normans. He was killed in the following year in the Battle of Monthechin.

Duncan II overthrew his uncle, Donald III, with English help but Donald regained the throne when Duncan was killed in battle or, perhaps, murdered by Edmund.

Edgar

must know

Born: c.1073
Parents: Malcolm III and Margaret
Ascended the throne: October 1097
Reign: Nine years
Married: Unmarried
Children: None
Died: 8 January 1107
Buried: Dunfermline Abbey

King Edgar

Helped to the throne by the English, Edgar admitted many Anglo-Norman settlers to Scotland and acknowledged William II of England as overlord. He formally ceded Kintyre and the Hebrides to King Magnus 'Barelegs' of Norway, who already occupied those territories.

He died unmarried and childless and was buried at Dunfermline Abbey, Fife.

Alexander I

must know	did you know?
Born: c.1078-80 **Parents:** Malcolm III and Margaret **Ascended the throne:** 8 January 1107 **Reign:** 17 years **Married:** Sybilla, illegitimate daughter of Henry I of England **Children:** No legitimate children **Died:** Stirling Castle, April 1124 **Buried:** Dunfermline Abbey	Alexander championed the independence of the Scottish church, which involved him in struggles with both of the English metropolitan sees. The historian John of Fordun said that he 'was humble and courteous to the clergy, but, to the rest of his subjects, terrible beyond measure.'

Alexander I ruled over a limited area, between the Forth and the Spey, making no attempt to control Ross and Argyll and leaving the south to his brother and successor, David I. The English connection grew stronger: Henry I was Alexander's father-in-law and brother-in-law (being married to Alexander's sister) as well as his overlord.

David I

must know	did you know?
Born: c.1084 **Parents:** Malcolm III and Margaret **Ascended the throne:** April 1124 **Reign:** 29 years **Married:** Matilda, daughter of the Earl of Huntingdon **Children:** Two sons, two daughters **Died:** Carlisle, 24 May 1153 **Buried:** Dunfermline Abbey	After a narrowly escaping English capture in Winchester in 1141, David returned to Scotland. He then remained in his own kingdom and devoted himself to its political and ecclesiastical reorganization. A devoted son of the church, he founded five bishoprics and many monasteries.

The last and most able of the sons of Malcolm III, David I ruled southern Scotland on behalf of his brother Alexander I before his accession. He had been brought up in England and, as Prince of Cumbria and Earl of Huntingdon (through his wife), he was one of the most powerful of English barons as well as King of Scots. English influence was consolidated during David's long and unusually peaceful reign. A feudal system headed by Anglo-Norman barons was established, trade and urban life encouraged, and royal government strengthened. The king supported the Church, founding bishoprics and parishes and endowing abbeys such as Melrose and Kelso. David's intervention in the English civil wars of Stephen and Matilda led to the acquisition of part of Northumbria.

Royal authority hardly existed in the Highlands, and the Western Isles were still nominally Norwegian.

King David I

Malcolm IV

must know

Born: 20 March 1141
Parents: Henry, Earl of Northumberland, and Ada de Warenne
Ascended the throne: 12 June 1153
Reign: Twelve years
Married: Unmarried
Died: Jedburgh, 9 December 1165
Buried: Dunfermline Abbey

Grandson of David I, Malcolm IV came to the throne as a boy of eleven, and was soon forced to cede his grandfather's conquests in northern England to the powerful Henry II. Nor could he prevent the King of Norway sacking Aberdeen, or Somerled, ancestor of the Macdonald Lords of the Isles, sacking Glasgow.

David I and Malcolm IV

William I

must know

Born: c.1143
Parents: Henry, Earl of Northumberland, and Ada de Warenne
Ascended the throne: 9 December 1165
Reign: 49 years
Married: Ermengarde de Beaumont, daughter of an illegitimate daughter of Henry I of England
Children: One son, the future Alexander II, and three daughters
Died: Stirling Castle, 4 December 1214
Buried: Arbroath Abbey

A more formidable character than his brother, Malcolm IV, William I, known as the Lion, concluded an alliance with France – the beginning of the 'Auld Alliance' – against England. Defeated and captured, William was forced to accept humiliating terms from the English in the Treaty of Falaise (1174), but later retrieved Scottish independence by agreement with Richard I of England, initiating nearly a century of peace between the two kingdoms.

However, he failed to subjugate the rebellious Celtic south-west, or to assert his authority over the MacDougall Lords of Lorne and the Macdonald Lords of the Isles.

William I

Alexander II

must know

Born: 24 August 1198
Parents: William I and Ermengarde de Beaumont
Ascended the throne: 4 December 1214
Crowned: Scone, 6 December 1214
Reign: 35 years
Married: (1) Joan, daughter of King John of England, (2) Mary de Coucy
Children: With (2) one son, the future Alexander III; one illegitimate daughter
Died: Isle of Kerrara, 6 July 1249
Buried: Melrose Abbey

did you know?

Alexander's first wife Joan died in March, 1238 in Essex, and in the following year, 1239, Alexander remarried. His second wife was Mary de Coucy. The marriage took place on May 15, 1239, and produced one son, the future Alexander III, born in 1241. In 1249 Alexander II suffered a fever at the Isle of Kerrera in the Inner Hebrides, and died there.

On his accession to the throne at the age of sixteen, Alexander was approached by the English barons and asked for his support in their campaign against King John. He led an army across the border into the Northern districts and harried the King's supporters. After the death of John, Alexander continued to support struggles against the young Henry III – in particular the campaign led by Prince Louis of France. In 1237, however, Alexander agreed terms with Henry in the Treaty of York, where the Scottish king abandoned his house's claim to Northumbria in exchange for some English estates.

The threat of invasion by Henry in 1243 never materialised, due in part to the promp action of Alexander in anticipating the attack and in part to the disinclination of the English barons for war, and peace was made at Newcastle.

The other notable success of his reign was his expedition against the dissidents in Argyllshire and the islands, where the inhabitants were known to be unsupportive of the Scottish rule and to be encouraging rebellion. The Western Isles still owed a nominal allegiance to Norway. His efforts to assert royal authority in the west, though, had limited success and were ended by his death on campaign. He had planned to sail to Argyll to enter negotiations with the Lord of Argyll, to press him to sever his allegiance to the Norwegain king, but on the way he suffered a fever at the Isle of Kerrera in the Inner Hebrides, and died there in 1249.

Alexander III

must know

Born: 4 September 1241
Parents: Alexander II and Mary de Coucy
Ascended the throne: 8 July 1249
Crowned: Scone, 13 July 1249
Reign: 37 years
Married: (1) Margaret, daughter of Henry III of England, (2) Yolande, daughter of the Comte de Dreux (1285)
Children: With (1), Margaret, Alexander and David
Died: Near Burntisland, Fife, 19 March 1286
Buried: Dunfermline Abbey

Alexander III continued his father's efforts to establish royal authority in the west. In 1263 he defeated Haakon of Norway at the Battle of Largs, and subsequently ended for ever the centuries-old rivalry between the royal houses of Scotland and Norway, although the Hebrides, while exchanging overlords, remained virtually independent under the Lords of the Isles. Otherwise, his reign was a period of comparative peace and growing prosperity.

Riding towards Kinghorn in Fife at night, his horse fell and he died from his injuries. All his children predeceased him. At his death, his heir was his three-year-old granddaughter Margaret, the 'Maid of Norway.'

Alexander III

Margaret

Born: Early in 1283
Parents: King Erik II of Norway and Margaret, daughter of Alexander III
Ascended the throne: 19 March 1286
Reign: Four years, five months
Died: At sea, September 1290
Buried: Bergen, Norway

The three-year-old Margaret ascended to the throne under a regency of six nobles. It was feared that Margaret, known as the 'Maid of Norway', as a young and powerless queen, would incite civil war between rival claimants, and so she was betrothed to the son of Edward I of England in return for an assurance of Scottish independence. Margaret died, aged seven, on the voyage from Norway to Scotland. She was the first Queen Regnant of Scots, and the last member of her dynasty.

First Interregnum

The death of the Maid of Norway left Scotland without an obvious heir to the throne. In this political vacuum, the most important figure was the powerful King Edward I of England. In 1290 he was asked to decide who should be king from among 13 competitors.

Of the two outstanding candidates, both of them Anglo-Norman lords who had fought in the English army, Edward chose John Balliol as likely to prove more amenable than his rival, Robert le Brus.

Robert Bruce, from the Seton Armorial

John

must know

Born: c.1249
Parents: Hugh de Balliol of Barnard Castle and Devorguilla of Galloway, a great-granddaughter of David I
Ascended the throne: 17 November 1292
Crowned: Scone, 30 November 1292
Reign: Four years
Married: Isabella de Warenne, a granddaughter of King John of England
Children: Two sons, Edward and Henry, and one or two daughters
Died: Normandy, 1313

Following his selection of John Balliol as King of Scots, Edward treated Scotland as a vassal state, and humiliated his appointee. John was known as 'Toom Tabard', meaning 'empty garment' or 'puppet'. and was reputedly a weak character under the dominance of his English overlord. But John finally stood up for himself and rebelled in 1296 and, fortified by a French alliance, invaded England. Edward launched a counter-invasion, supported by Bruce, later Robert I, and others of his Scottish vassals, and so commenced the Wars of Independence. John was defeated, forced to abdicate and, after a spell in prison, retired to his estates in Normandy.

Second Interregnum

Edward conquered Scotland and extracted homage from the chief landholders, who acknowledged him as king at Berwick in 1296. National resistance broke out in 1297, led by William Wallace, who argued that he and his supporters were acting on behalf of King John, since his abdication was invalid as obtained under duress. Although rebellions in Scotland continued over the years, this claim looked increasingly tenuous as John made no atttempt to extend support to the Scots. Effectively Scotland was left without a monarch until the accession of Robert the Bruce in 1306. Wallace was captured and executed in 1305, but the struggle for independence was renewed when some of Edward's chief Scottish vassals, including Robert the Bruce, turned against him.

Robert I and the Wars of Independence

Robert I, usually known as Robert the Bruce, was one of Scotland's greatest warrior-kings, and led Scotland to independence from England in 1328. He claimed the Scottish throne as a great-great-great-great grandson of David I.

---

must know

Born: Writtle, Essex, 11 July 1274
Parents: Robert le Brus, Lord of Annandale, and Margaret (Marjorie), daughter of Neil, Earl of Carrick
Crowned: Scone, 27 March 1306
Reign: 23 years. Married: (1) Isabella, daughter of the Earl of Mar, (2) Elizabeth de Burgh, daughter of the Earl of Ulster
Children: With (1), a daughter, Marjorie; with (2), two sons, including David II, and two daughters
Died: Cardross Castle, 7 June 1329
Buried: Dunfermline Abbey
(his heart at Melrose Abbey)

In 1306, Robert the Bruce and Red John Comyn, rival claimants to the Scottish Crown, met in a church in Dumfries. They quarrelled and Bruce killed Comyn. The act antagonized both the powerful Comyn family and the Church. Bruce nevertheless had himself crowned king at Scone. His position, already weak, became desperate when Edward I sent an army which defeated him at Methven in 1306. He became an outlaw on the run.

The tomb of Robert Bruce

Scottish recovery

A later legend relates how Bruce, hiding out in a cave, was inspired to renew resistance to the English after watching a spider, which, having tried and failed to attach its thread to a beam six times, refused to give up and was rewarded by success on the seventh attempt.

After Methven, there followed eight years of exhausting but deliberate refusal to meet the English on even ground. Such militaristic determination has caused many to consider Bruce as one of the great guerilla leaders in any age. In spite of further defeats, his supporters, including leaders of future clans – Donald, Campbell and Maclean – increased. After Edward I's death in 1307, his weaker son, Edward II, abandoned the Scottish campaign. Bruce was able to retake English-held strongpoints and even invade England. The decisive act was played at

Bannockburn, near Stirling, on 24 June 1314, when Bruce won a dramatic victory over Edward II's invading army.

The English knights were bogged down in marshy ground beside the Bannock burn, with the Scots above them. Edward's army fled, leaving the burn choked with English corpses. The war dragged on for 14 years, with the Scots now on the offensive. By the Treaty of Northampton (1328), the young Edward III abandoned English claims on Scotland.

Bruce at Bannockburn

David II

Born: Dunfermline, 5 March 1324
Parents: Robert I and Elizabeth de Burgh
Ascended the throne: 7 June 1329
Crowned: Scone, 24 November 1331
Reign: 41 years, with interruptions
Married: (1) Joan, daughter of Edward II of England, (2) Margaret Drummond
Children: None
Died: Edinburgh Castle, 22 February 1371
Buried: Holyrood Abbey

Owing to the victory of Edward III of England and his protégé, Edward Balliol, at Halidon Hill in July 1333, David and his queen were sent for safety into France, reaching Boulogne in May 1334. Little is known about the life of the Scottish king in France, except that Château-Gaillard was given to him for a residence by Philip VI.

The only surviving son of Robert Bruce, David II was driven into exile aged ten by Edward Balliol in 1334. Robert Stewart, Bruce's 17-year-old grandson, upheld his cause against Balliol and the English. David returned from France in 1341 and, responding to a French appeal for help, invaded England in 1346 and was captured at the Battle of Neville's Cross. He remained a prisoner in the English court until the Treaty of Berwick (1357) restored him in exchange for a ransom and a promise to make an English prince his heir.

David II

Edward

must know

Born: Unknown
Parents: King John Balliol and Isabella de Warenne
Crowned: Scone, 24 September 1332
Reign: Four years, with interruptions
Married: Unmarried
Died: Probably at Wheatley, Yorkshire, January 1367

did you know?

In January 20, 1356, Balliol surrendered his claim to the Scottish throne to Edward III in exchange for an English pension. He spent the rest of his life living in obscurity. He died in 1367, but the location of his grave is unknown.

Edward Balliol was the English candidate in the complex Scottish-English-French power struggle. He was deposed by the adherents of David II in December 1332, restored in 1333, deposed again in 1334, restored in 1335 and finally deposed in 1341. He left his claim to the Scottish Crown to Edward III of England.

The House of Stewart

The Scots rejected David II's promise to hand over the kingdom to the English, and the Crown passed to the former regent, Robert Stewart, whose surname derived from his father's office of High Steward of Scotland. Eventually, instead of English kings ruling the Scots, Stewart kings were to reign in England, though the members of this long-lasting dynasty were of highly variable monarchical abilities. Many of the early Stewart kings succeeded as young children, creating a power vacuum exploited by the great nobles.

Edward's royal seal

Robert II

> **must know**
>
> **Born:** Paisley, 2 March 1316
> **Parents:** Walter, High Steward of Scotland, and Marjorie, daughter of Robert I
> **Ascended the throne:** 22 February 1371
> **Crowned:** Scone, c.26 February 1371
> **Reign:** 19 years
> **Married:** (1) Elizabeth Mure, (2) Euphemia, daughter of the Earl of Ross
> **Children:** With (1), four sons and six daughters; with (2), two sons and two daughters; eight or more illegitimate children
> **Died:** Dundonald Castle, 19 April 1390
> **Buried:** Scone

Robert II was less effective as king than he had been as regent for David II. Conflict between Crown and nobility became a major disruptive force in Scottish government, lasting for centuries.

Robert III

> **must know**
>
> **Born:** c.1337 (christened 'John')
> **Parents:** Robert II and Elizabeth Mure
> **Ascended the throne:** 19 April 1390
> **Crowned:** Scone, c.14 August 1390
> **Reign:** 16 years
> **Married:** Annabella Drummond of Stobhall
> **Children:** Three sons and four daughters; one illegitimate son
> **Died:** 4 April 1406
> **Buried:** Paisley Abbey

> **did you know?**
>
> Fearing for the safety of his eldest son, James, Robert had him hidden at Dirleton Castle, with a view to smuggling him from there to France. However, a month later, in 1406, Englishmen captured the young James en route. King Robert died soon after, probably at Rothesay, and allegedly died grief over the capture of James.

Robert III had been crippled by a horse and virtually abdicated in 1399. The regency was disputed between his son David, Duke of Rothesay, and his brother Robert, Duke of Albany. Rothesay was kidnapped and mudered in 1402, leaving Albany supreme.

James I

Born: Dunfermline, December 1394
Parents: Robert III and Annabella Drummond
Ascended the throne: 4 April 1406
Crowned: Scone, May 1424
Reign: 20 years
Married: Joan (or Jane) Beaufort, daughter of the Earl of Somerset and great-granddaughter of Edward III of England
Children: Two sons, including James II, and six daughters
Died: Perth, 21 February 1437
Buried: Perth

James was captured by the English in 1406 and held hostage until ransomed in 1424. During his absence, the Duke of Albany and, after his death in 1420, his son Murdoch, held power as regents.

During the regency the great nobles built up their power and independence. The Macdonald Lords of the Isles maintained total autonomy. Invading Islesmen sacked Aberdeen in 1411 but retreated after a bloody battle with Albany's allies at Harlaw.

James's vigorous but vindictive reforming policies made him unpopular, and he was assassinated by kinsmen.

James I

James II

must know

Born: Holyrood Abbey, 16 October 1430
Parents: James I and Joan Beaufort
Ascended the throne: 21 February 1437
Crowned: Kelso Abbey, 25 March 1437
Reign: 23 years
Married: Mary, daughter of the Duke of Gueldres
Children: Four sons, including James III, and two daughters
Died: Roxburgh, 3 August 1460
Buried: Holyrood Abbey

did you know?

James II was known as 'Fiery Face' because of a conspicuous vermilion birthmark on his face. Inheriting the throne at the age of six, most of his reign saw the government in the hands of others. He had six sisters, who were married into the royal dynasties of Europe.

After another troublesome minority, James II assumed control in 1449 and took strong action to quell the disruptive nobility. The mighty Douglasses were broken when their leaders were invited to dinner with the young king in 1440 and murdered. Their successor was killed by James himself in 1452. While besieging Roxburgh, held by the English, a gun exploded and killed him.

James II

James III

must know

Born: St Andrews (?Stirling), probably in May 1452
Parents: James II and Mary of Gueldres
Ascended the throne: 3 August 1460
Crowned: Kelso Abbey, 10 August 1460
Reign: 28 years
Married: Margaret of Denmark, daughter of the King of Denmark, Norway and Sweden
Children: Three sons, including James IV
Died: Milltown, near Stirling, 11 June 1488
Buried: Cambuskenneth Abbey

The dowry of James III's wife, Margaret, included sovereignty of the Northern and Western Isles. After another regency, James took control in 1469. He was more of a

scholar than a warlord, and his efforts to assert royal authority provoked rebellions and an English invasion. His brothers, whom he had imprisoned, joined his opponents. One, the Duke of Albany, was proclaimed King of Scots after escaping to London. A later conspiracy set up James's own son as king. James confronted the rebels at Sauchieburn (1488) and was hurt during the battle when his horse threw him. A man masquerading as a priest stabbed him to death.

James III

James IV

must know

Born: 17 March 1473
Parents: James III and Margaret of Denmark
Ascended the throne: 11 June 1488
Crowned: Scone, 26 June 1488
Reign: 25 years
Married: Margaret Tudor, daughter of Henry VII of England
Children: Four sons, including James V, and two daughters; seven illegitimate children
Died: Flodden Field, 9 September 1513
Buried: Possibly Sheen Abbey, Surrey; his head, possibly, in St Michael's Church, Wood Street, London

The most distinguished member of his dynasty, James IV was a Renaissance prince, a patron of the arts, energetic, intelligent – he spoke Gaelic among other languages – and a born leader. For the first time in a century, there was no minority. James crushed the rebels and re-established royal authority, presiding over unprecedented economic growth, educational and artistic development and cultivated town life. The Lordship of the Isles was ended but James's goodwill visit in 1494 had disappointing results, so he resorted to tougher policies, relying on feudal magnates like the Campbell Earl of Argyll.

James saw the importance of Scotland having a large navy. He acquired 38 ships for the Royal Scottish Navy and founded two new dockyards. His flagship, launched in 1511, was the *Great Michael* and was then the largest ship in Europe.

For a time he supported the pretender to the English throne Perkin Warbeck and carried out a brief invasion of England on his behalf. But, having fought off the aggression of Henry VII, James recognized that peace between Scotland and England was in the interests of both countries, and so agreed a treaty of 'perpetual peace' in 1502, and cemented relations further by marrying Henry's daughter, Margaret Tudor.

When war broke out between England and France, James found himself in a difficult position. The new king of England, Henry VIII, attempted to invade France in 1513, and James, hoping to take advantage of Henry's absence, led an invading army southward, only to be killed at the disastrous Battle of Flodden Field.

James IV

Flodden

When France was attacked by a European coalition that included England, she appealed for help to her only ally, Scotland. James IV realized that the defeat of France would put Scotland in danger.

He earned the name 'Rex Pacificator', or King-Peacemake', for his efforts to mediate between England, to which he was allied by his marriage to Henry VIII's sister, and France, Scotland's 'auld ally'. His efforts to prevent war were rejected by Henry VIII, who defiantly declared that he was the 'verie owner' of Scotland. On 22 August 1513, at the head of the finest army Scotland had ever produced, James crossed the Tweed into England.

He was backed by one of the largest armies ever assembled by a Scots monarch, roughly 30,000 men, and they marched south across the border and occupied four strategically important castles. The English force was somewhat smaller, comprising about 20,000 men, and was commanded by Thomas Howard, Earl of Surrey.

The Scots met the English army near Flodden Edge on a stormy September afternoon. James's forces were in an extremely strong position from which the English would find it difficult to prise them. The Earl of Surrey therefore marched his men rapidly round the Scots' position, forcing them to turn round to face their attackers. While this manoeuvre took place the English hammered the Scots with long-range artillery and the English archers poured down fire. James had planned to fight a defensive rather than a much more dangerous and exposed offensive battle, but the English bombardments ruined his plans.

The battle soon resolved itself into a series of charges by the Scots and a melée of desperate hand-to-hand fighting that caused numerous casualties on both sides. The bills of the English soldiers proved better weapons than Scottish spears. The Scots refused to give way, and the battle turned into a dreadful massacre that lasted four hours until nightfall obliged the combatants to break off. Scots casualties were extremely heavy, roughly 10,000. Scotland's ruling class was decimated. Among the dead were the king, nine earls, 14 lords and many chiefs of Highland clans.

James IV died excommunicate, and Henry VIII (who was in France at the time of Flodden) had to get the Pope's permission to have him buried in consecrated ground. There were many who believed that the king was not dead – but had perhaps escaped to France – and would one day return.

James V

Born: Linlithgow Palace, c.10 April 1512
Parents: James IV and Margaret Tudor
Ascended the throne: 9 September 1513
Crowned: Stirling Castle, 21 September 1513
Reign: 29 years
Married: (1) Madeleine, daughter of Francis I of France, (2) Mary, daughter of the Duke of Guise
Children: With (1), two sons and one daughter, Mary, future Queen of Scots; nine illegitimate children
Died: Falkland Palace, 14 December 1542
Buried: Holyrood Abbey

In the days of the infant king, Scotland was devastated by the results of Flodden and by internal intrigues. Two main factions arose: the pro-English and (eventually) Protestant; and the pro-French and Catholic.

In 1528 James V escaped from the control of the pro-English faction. Taking over the royal government, he had some success in restoring order, even in the north and west. He married a French rather than an English princess (the first soon died but he married another), resulting in war with the aggressive Henry VIII. Defeated at Solway Moss (1542), he died soon after the birth of his hoped-for heir – a girl.

James V

Mary

must know

Born: Linlithgow Palace, 7 December 1542
Parents: James V and Mary of Guise
Ascended the throne: 14 December 1542
Crowned: Stirling, 9 September 1543
Reign: 20 years
Married: (1) Francis II of France (1558), (2) Henry Stewart, Lord Darnley (1565), (3) James Hepburn, Earl of Bothwell (1567)
Children: With (2), one son, James VI and I
Died: Fotheringhay Castle, Northamptonshire, 8 February 1587
Buried: Peterborough Cathedral; removed to Westminster Abbey in 1612

In 1544 Henry VIII of England invaded Scotland in an effort to enforce the marriage of the infant Mary to his son Edward. She was sent to France to marry the Dauphin, later Francis II. A Catholic, she returned to Scotland, which was now predominantly

Protestant, after Francis's death in 1561 and married her unruly cousin, Lord Darnley. They fell out, and Darnley was involved in the plot to murder her secretary, David Rizzio. He was himself killed in 1567. Mary scandalized her subjects by promptly marrying her presumed lover and the suspected murderer of Darnley, the raffish Earl of Bothwell. Forced to abdicate, she fled to England, where she was held prisoner by Elizabeth I. A focus for pro-Catholic intrigue, she was executed 19 years later.

Mary, Queen of Scots

James VI

Born: Edinburgh, 19 June 1566
Parents: Mary, Queen of Scots, and Lord Darnley
Ascended the throne: 24 July 1567
Crowned: Stirling, 29 July 1567
Reign: 58 years
Married: Anne, daughter of Frederick II of Denmark (1589)
Children: Three sons and five daughters
Died: Theobalds Park, Hertfordshire, 27 March 1625
Buried: Westminster Abbey

did you know?

James is considered to have been one of the most intellectual and learned monarchs. He was a talented scholar and wrote works such as *The True Law of Free Monarchies* (1594) and *A Counterblaste to Tobacco* (1604).

James VI was proclaimed king at the age of one on the forced abdication of his mother. He had a wretched childhood while Scotland was ruled by a succession of regents, and became the puppet of different factions. In 1583, escaping from the captivity of the dominant Protestant lords, James asserted his authority and took over the government, though he was unable to control the strife of the fractious nobility, Protestant or Catholic, or to subdue Presbyterianism, which he regarded as a threat to royal government.

He was, however, one of Scotland's most successful monarchs and was a notoriously shrewd political operator. He ruled his country very effectively, and by the end of the 16th century, his control stretched as far as the Highlands. He maintained good relations with England (in spite of the execution of his mother), and in 1603 he inherited the English Crown on the death of Elizabeth I (see James I of England, page 151).

James VI

The Union of the Crowns

By 1583, when the 17-year-old James VI took over his royal powers in Scotland, it was obvious that Elizabeth I of England would produce no heir, and England's Tudor dynasty would end with her death.

As her successor, James was really the only likely candidate. He was directly descended from Henry VII (founder of the Tudor dynasty) and, vitally important, he was a Protestant. Elizabeth's father, Henry VIII, had feared that the English Crown would go to a Scot: in his will, he excluded Margaret Tudor, James's grandmother, and her descendants from the line of succession. Although technically excluded by the will, which, under an Act of Parliament, had the force of law, both Mary and James were serious claimants to the English Crown, as they were Elizabeth's closest relatives.

In 1586, Mary was implicated in the Babington Plot, a scheme which sought to put a Catholic queen on the throne of England having murdered the Protestant Elizabeth. Elizabeth had previously spared Mary's life after implications in earlier plots, but could no longer tolerate the danger she posed. Consequently, Mary was executed for her crimes in 1587. But for the will of Henry VIII, James was now the Heir Presumptive to the English Crown.

The execution of Mary, Queen of Scots

James could not wait for Elizabeth to die. In private, he complained that she seemed likely to outlive the sun and moon. He was nevertheless careful to stay on good terms with England and its queen. The execution of his mother, Mary, enraged her former subjects, but James made only a formal protest.

Elizabeth refused to discuss the succession, and ignored broad hints from James that she should name him, but all her courtiers favoured James. Her powerful minister, Sir Robert Cecil, Earl of Salisbury, kept up a secret correspondence with him, offering advice and encouragement. It was reported that Elizabeth did eventually name James as her heir, on her deathbed, and thus, despite her earlier reluctance, helped to ensure a peaceful succession.

Early reign in England

James was an extravagant spender; only the skill of his advisors could avert financial disaster. James also embroiled himself in numerous conflicts with Parliament. Being accustomed to a timid Parliament of Scotland, he did not like working with its more aggressive English counterpart. Before his accession to the English throne, he had written *The True Law of Free Monarchies*, in which he argued that the divine right of kings was sanctioned by the apostolic succession, and which illustrates James's difficulty in sharing the power of his government.

Though James was careful to accept Catholics in his realm, many of his subjects did not know his policies, only that he had an extreme Protestant background, and there were a number of plots to remove him from power. In 1605, a group of Catholic extremists led by Robert Catesby developed a plan, known as the Gunpowder Plot, to blow up the chamber of the House of Lords, where the king and members of Parliament would be gathered for the State Opening. However information regarding the plot was leaked and Guy Fawkes, one of the conspirators, was catured and tortured until he revealed the identities of the other conspirators. James subsequently took care to not to strongly enforce anti-Catholic doctrine, and there were no more plots after 1605.

One Crown, two governments

The union of the Scottish and English Crowns was just that – one king but two kingdoms. Except for sharing a monarch, England and Scotland were to remain separate until the Act of Union in 1707.

Irish Kings

Ireland was probably settled by Celts soon after 500 BC. The Greek explorer Pytheas, who circumnavigated Britain in the late fourth century BC, suggests that the Celts were certainly in possession by that time. There seems to have been a rebellion against them by the original inhabitants in the first century AD.

The **Romans** never conquered Ireland, although they had substantial outposts on the eastern coast. Archaeology has revealed considerable Romanization, deriving mainly, perhaps, from post-Roman Britain.

From an early date, the Irish tribes were ruled by royal dynasties, supported by an aristocratic élite. Thanks to the ancient Irish interest in genealogy, hundreds of names of kings and dynasties are known, but they remain just names, some no doubt legendary.

There may have been about 100 petty kingdoms in Ireland at any given time. The king was essentially a war leader and representative of his people.

Real power belonged to the kings of the provinces, who were constantly engaged in war and dynastic conflicts.

There were five provinces, or kingdoms, the so-called 'Five Fifths', roughly corresponding to their modern descendants: Ulster; Connacht; North Leinster; South Leinster; and Munster. After AD c.500, there were seven, Ulster forming three kingdoms, together with Meath (occupying most of North Leinster), Leinster, Munster and Connacht.

On the evidence of the old sagas, a concept of Irish unity existed at a very early period, with the Kings of Connacht and Ulster contending for supreme authority. In the third century AD, the Kings of Connacht gained the upper hand, expanding east and north and making Tara their capital. The semi-legendary figure of **Cormac** (reigned c.227-66) played a leading role in their expansion.

King Cormac and Eithne

As Roman authority declined in the fourth century AD, Irish raids on the coast of Britain became more frequent, and led to settlement. Colonies were founded in Wales and – a permanent occupation – in Scotland (by the Scots of Dalriada).

The greatest leader of the House of Conn (from which Connacht took its name) was the semi-legendary **Niall of the Nine Hostages** (reigned c.380-405). He and his kin, the Ui ('descendants of') Niall ruled almost all the northern half of Ireland. One group, the northern Ui Neill, controlled western Ulster; another, the southern Ui Neill, were based in Meath. The Dal Cuinn ('race of Conn') provided the High Kings of Ireland until the early eleventh century.

The Vikings

The name Viking is a borrowed word from the native Scandanavian term for the Norse warriors who raided the coasts of Scandanavia, the British Isles, and other parts of Europe from the late 7th century to the 11th century. The Vikings made their incursions westwards, and Varangians roamed the lands to the east.

Norse raids began in 795, and in the ninth century Norsemen founded a number of small coastal kingdoms, forming the nucleus of future cities such as Dublin, Wexford and Waterford. Norse rulers used their Irish kingdoms to launch attacks on England and Scotland.

The Norse invasions halted in the reign of the high king **Aed Finnliath** (862-79). He extinguished all the Norse outposts in northern Ireland, but the Norse Kings of Dublin, such as **Olaf the White**, dominated a large part of the country in the ninth century, sometimes preventing the high king from holding his annual assembly at Tara.

Brian Boru killed by Vikings

The threat of a Norse conquest was ended by **Brian Boru** (941-1014), Ireland's greatest national hero. He became King of Munster in 976 and in 999 gained the support of the Kings of Leinster and Dublin, after defeating them in battle at Glen Mama, near Dublin. In 1002 he became high king, displacing **Mael Sechnaill III**, the last of the Ui Neill high kings.

The dissatisfied Kings of Leinster and Dublin formed a conspiracy with Sigurd, the Norse Earl of Orkney, who landed with a large Norse army at Clontarf, near Dublin, in 1014. Brian was expecting him, and the Norsemen with their Leinster allies were utterly defeated. After the battle, however, a Norse warrior entered Brian's tent and killed him.

Brian had no worthy successor. Mael Sechnaill regained the high kingship until his death in 1022, but thereafter, for 150 years, Ireland's minor kings battled for supremacy, and no high king gained universal recognition or reigned without a rival.

The Normans

In 1166 the unpopular King of Leinster, **Dermot MacMurrough** (reigned 1134-71) was driven out by a coalition of enemies. With his daughter Eva, he sailed to England to seek help. The English king, Henry II, gave permission for him to raise forces, and he soon enlisted ambitious Norman adventurers in South Wales. Chief among them was Richard de Clare, Earl of Pembroke, known as **Strongbow** (died 1176), who was promised Eva in marriage. Dermot returned to Ireland in 1169, soon followed by his Norman allies.

The invaders quickly achieved success, when a force under the last High King of Ireland, **Rory O'Connor** (Ruadri Ua Conchobar, reigned 1166-86, died 1198), was defeated. On Dermot's death, Strongbow, now married to Eva, declared himself King of Leinster.

The Normans had a profound effect on Irish culture, history and ethnicity. While initially the Normans in the 12th century kept themselves as a distinct culture and ethnicity, they were quickly subsumed into Ireland, and it is often said that they became more Irish than the Irish themselves. The Normans settled mostly in an area east of Ireland, later known as the Pale, and also built many fine castles and settlements, including Trim Castle and Dublin Castle. Both cultures intermixed, borrowing from each other's language, culture and outlook.

Fearing the creation of an independent Norman kingdom in Ireland, Henry II arrived in person in 1171 to assert his authority. He brought a large army but did not need it. In general, the Irish chiefs received him with relief. Rory O'Connor recognized him as overlord in 1176, though he was later deposed. **Cathal O'Connor**, King of Connacht (1201-24), the last native Irish king, resisted the English for some years. English rule in the Middle Ages was nominal. Ireland continued to be ruled by local nobles and chiefs, who acknowledged the King of England as their overlord but never set eyes on him.

Henry VIII was the first English king to call himself 'King of Ireland'. Thereafter, English interference steadily increased, and was increasingly resented, until Ireland won independence. Twenty-six counties formed the Irish Free State in 1922; 6 northern counties formed Northern Ireland which remained part of the UK. The Free State became a republic and left the Commonwealth in 1947.

Richard II & Four Kings of Ireland

Major Welsh Rulers

The Romans invaded Wales in the first century ad, conquering the Silures (in South Wales) and the Ordovices (in North and Mid-Wales) as well as lesser Celtic tribes. Only South Wales, however, became fully part of the Roman world. Elsewhere, forts were scattered across the country, and many of them were abandoned before the final Roman withdrawal from Britain.

Because Wales is a mountainous country, communications were difficult, presenting many obstacles to invaders but also making it difficult for defenders to assemble – and feed – an army. The kingdoms that developed in the early Middle Ages were therefore small and separate. The necessary preconditions for the formation of a single, nationwide political unit did not exist.

However, as time passed, some of the small kingdoms that emerged after the Roman period proved more successful than others. The most viable were those that commanded stretches of useful lowland, especially Gwynedd in the north (where rugged Snowdonia protected the 'bread-basket' of Anglesey), Dyfed in the south-west and Deheubarth in the south. Powys, in the east, was also a survivor, but suffered by its proximity to England.

Significantly, the great princes of medieval Wales were all westerners, many from Gwynedd. They were able to exercise authority well beyond the borders of their kingdoms and at times claimed to rule all Wales.

These were individual triumphs, which hardly lasted more than one generation, for there was no law of primogeniture to prevent the division of a chief's territory among his heirs. Yet the three dominant kingdoms continued to form the basic political framework until the English conquest.

With the Normans came the opportunity for rulers to learn new methods. The Welsh began to build castles and have mounted knights, In particular, they saw virtue in the new monastic orders.

In 1282 the conqueror of Wales, King Edward I of England, declared his own new-born son 'Prince of Wales', a title still bestowed on the heir to the British Crown. Sporadic resistance to English rule culminated in the rebellion of **Owain Glyndwr** in 1400. Henry Tudor, whose ancestors included a daughter of Llywelyn the Great, gained the English throne as Henry VII in 1485, and England and Wales were merged in one kingdom by the Act of Union (1536).

Cunedda

A British chieftain from, possibly, Lothian, Cunedda and his kin settled in North Wales after driving out the Scots (invaders from Ireland). The Kings of Gwynedd claimed him as their ancestor.

Maelgwyn Hir, 'the Tall'

did you know?

Before the Anglo-Saxon invasions of Britain in the 6th and 7th centuries, there was no such place as England and no English language. Welsh was in fact the native language throughout all areas of what is now England.

Allegedly a grandson of Cunedda, Maelgwyn Hir ruled most of North Wales, including Anglesey, from his stronghold at Degannwy. Though said to have entered a monastery, he soon returned to society, and gained an unsavoury reputation: he was believed to have murdered his wife and nephew in order to marry the latter's widow.

Cadwallon

did you know?

If 'England' didn't exist, neither did Wales. It was the name given to the area of land that now forms Wales by the Anglo-Saxon newcomers, who called the native Welsh 'waelas', meaning 'foreigner'.

Driven out by the Northumbrian king, Edwin of Deira, Cadwallon formed an alliance with King Penda of Mercia, regained his kingdom and defeated and killed Edwin at Heathfield, near Doncaster. He failed to make the most of this opportunity to restore British (Celtic) rule and was killed by Edwin's kinsman, Oswald of Bernicia, in a sneak attack near Hadrian's Wall.

Merfyn Frych, 'the Freckled'

must know

Authority: King of Gwynedd
Reigned: 825-44
Married: Nest, daughter of the King of Powys
Died: 844

Merfyn Frych inherited Anglesey in 825 and was later recognized as king throughout much of North Wales.

Rhodri Mawr, 'the Great'

must know

Authority: King of Gwynedd
Reigned: 844-78
Parents: Merfyn Frych and Nest
Married: Angharad, daughter of the King of Ceredigion (Deheubarth)
Died: 878

He succeeded his father as King of Gwynedd, his uncle as King of Powys (855) and his father-in-law as King of Ceredigion (Deheubarth), thus uniting most of Wales outside Dyfed and Gwent. Although his dominion did not last, it encouraged the idea of Welsh unity among future generations. Rhodri's reign was prosperous, but he spent much of his life fighting, especially against Viking marauders. He was killed in battle against the Mercians.

Anarawd ap Rhodri

must know

Authority: Prince of Gwynedd
Reigned: 878-916
Parents: Rhodri Mawr and Angharad
Died: 916

did you know?

Due to the scarcity of historical records, very little is known about the early Welsh rulers. Much of what has survived is full of contradiction, and often the facts have been manipulated and distorted in the name of propaganda and legend.

Rhodri Mawr's lands were divided on his death, Anarawd receiving part of Gwynedd, including Anglesey. He may have been responsible for a defeat inflicted on the Mercians in 881: he later formed a defensive alliance with the Danish King of York. In campaigns against his brother **Cadell ap Rhodri**, who ruled Ceredigion, he received aid from Alfred of Wessex, whom he acknowledged as overlord. Later rulers of Gwynedd and Deheubarth were descended from Anarawd and Cadell respectively.

Hywel Dda, 'the Good'

must know

Authority: King of Deheubarth
Reigned: c.904-50
Father: Cadell ap Rhodri
Married: Elen, daughter of the King of Dyfed
Died: 950

Hywel Dda inherited Ceredigion (Deheubarth) on his father's death, gained Dyfed by his marriage and, when Idwal Foel (see below) was killed in 942, he took over Gwynedd too. Thus, most of Wales was united, though briefly, under him. He seems to have been a frequent visitor to the court of the House of Wessex and acknowledged the English king as overlord. No mere warlord, he was something of a scholar, who made a pilgrimage to Rome, minted his own silver coinage and compiled a code of law, after first summoning a consultative assembly from all over his territory. His laws contributed to the consciousness of national unity.

Idwal Foel, 'the Bald'

must know

Authority: King of Gwynedd
Reigned: 916-42
Father: Anarawd ap Rhodri
Died: 942

A reluctant vassal, Idwal Foel was killed in a rebellion against the English, and his kingdom passed to his nephew, Hywel Dda (see above).

Iago ap Idwal

must know

Authority: King of Gwynedd
Reigned: 950-79
Father: Idwal Foel
Died: ?979

Excluded from the kingdom when his father died, he regained it, in conjunction with his brother Ieuaf, on the death of Hywel Dda. Complex dynastic conflicts ended with Iago being deposed by Ieuaf's son. Iago was one of the Welsh princes recorded as paying homage to the English king, Edgar, at Chester in 973.

Maredudd ap Owain ap Hywel Dda

must know

Authority: King of Deheubarth
Reigned: 986-99
Died: 999

Maredudd inherited Deheubarth from his father and emulated his grandfather in uniting, briefly, North and South Wales.

Llywelyn ap Seisyll

must know

Authority: King of Deheubarth and Gwynedd
Reigned: 1018-23
Married: Angharad, daughter of Maredudd ap Owain

Llywelyn had claims to Gwynedd and, through his marriage, Deheubarth. His warlike abilities made him master of both and, though his reign was short, he laid the basis for the claims of his son.

Gruffydd ap Llywelyn

did you know?

Not all the Welsh rulers are listed here due to the scarcity of historical records. Much of what we do know comes from the *Annales Cambriae*, a document that included the pedigrees of Welsh royal families.

must know

Authority: King of Gwynedd and Powys
Reigned: 1039-63
Parents: Llywelyn ap Seisyll and Angharad
Married: Ealgith, daughter of Aelfgar of Mercia

On succeeding his father, Gruffydd ap Llywelyn gained immediate fame by defeating the Mercians. He then turned against Deheubarth, whose king was defeated and killed. Gruffydd did not, however, gain complete control of the southern kingdom until 1055. He raided the English borders and formed an alliance with King Aelfgar of Mercia. In 1062, he was suddenly attacked by Earl Harold Godwinson of Wessex and killed by traitors.

Gruffydd ap Cynan

must know

Authority: King of Gwynedd
Reigned: 1081-1137
Born: c.1055
Parents: Cynan ap Iago and Rhagnell, daughter of the Norse King of Dublin
Married: Angharad, daughter of a Gwynedd chieftain
Died: 1137

Gruffydd ap Cynan was the son of a Welsh prince, Cynan ap Iago, and an Irish Viking mother. He was born in Ireland of the royal line of Gwynedd and made several attempts to regain Gwynedd before finally succeeding. During his lengthy reign, considered to be a 'Golden Age' for Wales, he retook much of Gwynedd from its English conquerors.

However, he was plagued by invaders of his own and much of his kingdom was overrun by Normans, who imprisoned him. He escaped to join the anti-Norman rebellion of 1094. Driven out again in 1098, he retired to Ireland, but returned as ruler of Anglesey, swearing fealty to Henry I.

Rhys ap Tewdwr

must know

Authority: King of Deheubarth
Reigned: 1081-1093
Married: Gwladys, daughter of the King of Powys
Died: 1093

did you know?

Rhys ap Tewdwr had two sons, Gruffydd and Hywel, and a daughter, Nest. She was a legendary beauty, and is sometimes known as the 'Helen of Wales', as her abduction from her husband started a civil war.

A descendant of Hywel Dda, Rhys ap Tewdwr made good his claim to the kingdom at the Battle of Mynydd Carn (1081) with the help of Gruffydd ap Cynan, and was confirmed in it by King William I of England, apparently paying £40 a year. He fought against various rival princes and rebellious kinsmen and, after William's death, was killed in battle against the Normans who were overruning South Wales.

Madog ap Maredudd

must know

Authority: King of Powys
Reigned: 1132-60
Father: Maredudd ap Bleddyn ap Cynfin
Married: Susanna, daughter of the King of Gwynedd
Died: 1160

did you know?

Madog died in 1160, and was buried in the church of St Tysilio at Meifod. Madog's eldest son, Llywelyn, was killed soon after his father's death and Powys was shared between a number of sons and nephews.

The last king of all Powys, Madog was forced to defend it against a prince of Gwynedd but maintained good relations with the Norman Earl of Chester and King Henry II of England.

The reign of Madog ap Maredudd in fact represented the most stable era in the history of the kingdom or principality of Powys. Powys was something of a buffer state between Gwynedd and England, and ruling it involved playing the one off against the other. Madog's valour and political skills were much praised by the poets and he features in the medieval tale, *Breuddwyd Rhonabwy* (*The Dream of Rhonabwy*). Following his death Powys was divided into Powys Wenwynwyn - the later county of Montgomery - and Powys Fadog - essentially the southern parts of the later counties of Denbigh and Flint. The kingdom was never reunited.

Owain Gwynedd

Authority: King of Gwynedd
Born: c.1100
Reigned: 1137-70
Parents: Gruffydd ap Cynan and Angharad
Married: (1) Gwladus, daughter of Llywarch ap Trahaern, King of Gwynedd, (2) Christina, a cousin
Children: Two sons by each wife; numerous other children
Died: 1170
Buried: Bangor Cathedral

The name Owain Gwynedd serves to prevent confusion with another Owain ap Gruffydd. With his brother he restored Gwynedd during his father's old age. He extended the kingdom and conducted fruitful operations in the south, benefiting from the anarchy in England. But when the English king, Henry II, appeared in North Wales in 1157, Owain Gwynedd recognized the need for prudence, swore fealty, and changed his title from king to prince. He joined the general rebellion against Henry in 1165, when his authority extended as far as the Dee.

Owain Gwynedd

Rhys ap Gruffydd, 'The Lord Rhys'

must know

Authority: King of Deheubarth
Born: c.1133
Reigned: 1155-97
Parents: Gruffydd ap Rhys ap Tewdwr and Gwenlliam, daughter of Gruffydd ap Cynan
Married: Gwenlan, daughter of Madog ap Maredudd
Children: Eight sons, one daughter
Died: 1197
Buried: St David's Cathedral

Rhys ap Gruffydd

Rhys ap Gruffydd took part in his first battle at the age of 13. He rendered homage reluctantly to Henry II of England in 1158, giving up some territory and the title of king – hence the name by which history knows him, 'The Lord Rhys'. He recouped his losses after the rebellion of 1165 when the most troublesome Normans were turning their attention to Ireland and Henry was having trouble with the Church. Reconciled with Henry, he remained on good terms and adopted Anglo-Norman customs. His later years were troubled by rebellious sons and Norman neighbours.

Llywelyn ap Iorwerth, 'the Great'

must know

Authority: Prince of Gwynedd
Born: Dolwyddelan Castle, Gwynedd, 1173
Reigned: 1194-1240
Parents: Iorwerth Drwyndwn, son of Owain Gwynedd, and Margaret, daughter of Madog ap Mareddud
Married: Joan, daughter of King John of England
Children: One son, four daughters; other illegitimate children
Died: 11 April 1240
Buried: Aberconwy Abbey

The early years of Llywelyn ap Iorweth were occupied, as was often the case, with dynastic conflicts. He gradually eliminated his rivals and showed his mettle by capturing Mold from the English (1199). By 1203 he was in undisputed control of all Gwynedd. Powys remained a potential threat, but within two years he had established his suzerainty (feudal lordship) there, at the same time seeking to nullify adverse reaction from England by marrying the illegitimate daughter of the king. Inevitably, friendship with England eventually broke down. He lost some territory in 1211, but was able to recoup as John became embroiled with his barons. Llywelyn co-operated with John's opponents, including the Pope, while bestowing his numerous daughters as wives on the Marcher lords. He extended his operations to south Wales, and was recognized as suzerain by all the Welsh princes. In the famous Magna Carta wrung out of King John by the barons in 1215, special clauses were concerned with securing the rights of Llywelyn. In his later years Llywelyn planned to adopt primogeniture to preserve his princedom and considered a centralized government.

Dafydd ap Llewelyn

must know

Authority: Prince of Wales
Born: c.1208
Reigned: 1240-1246
Parents: Llywelyn the Great and Joan
Married: Isabella, daughter of Williamde Breos, a Marcher lord
Children: None
Died: 25 February 1246
Buried: Aberconwy Abbey

did you know?

Dafydd's half-brother, Gruffydd ap Llewelyn, was imprisoned in the Tower of London. On St David's Day, 1244, he attempted to escape by climbing down a rope of sheets knotted together. The sheets broke, and Gruffydd plunged to his death, thus strengthening Dafydd's claim to the throne.

The generally recognized heir of Llywelyn the Great, Dafydd ap Llywelyn took the title 'Prince of Wales' in 1244. Relations with his English overlord were tense, but his position was strengthened when his rival, Gruffydd (an illegitimate half-brother), broke his neck escaping from prison. But Dafydd died young and without an heir, and his dominion was once more divided.

Llewelyn ap Gruffydd, 'Llywelyn the Last'

must know

Authority: Prince of Wales
Born: c.1225
Reigned: 1246-82
Parents: Gruffydd ap Llywelyn ap Iorwerth and Senena
Married: Eleanor de Montfort, daughter of Simon de Montfort, 6th Earl of Leicester
Children: One daughter
Died: 11 December 1282
Buried: Abbey of Cwm Hir

Llewelyn ap Gruffydd

Llywelyn ap Gruffydd defeated his brothers at Bryn Derwin (1255) and, seizing the opportunity of the barons' revolt (see Henry III, page 114-15), he made himself lord of as much territory as his grandfather, Llywelyn the Great, while forming an alliance with the barons' leader, Simon de Montfort. He was officially recognized as Prince of Wales by the Treaty of Montgomery (1267). The succession of Edward I to the Crown of England brought his ruin. He refused to offer homage to Edward and within a few years his sovereignty was confined to part of western Gwynedd. Renewing his rebellion in 1282, he was killed in a skirmish near Builth.

Owain Glyndwr

must know

Authority: 'Prince of Wales' (self-proclaimed)
Born: c.1354
Parents: Gruffydd Fychan ap Madog and Helen, daughter of Thomas ap Llywelyn
Married: Margaret Hanmer
Children: Six sons, several daughters
Died: c.1416

A descendant of Madog ap Maredudd and other princes, Owain Glyndwr led a revolt, originally sparked off by personal grievances, against King Henry IV of England in 1400. By 1405 he controlled most of Wales, holding parliaments and making treaties with foreign powers. He survived the fall of his chief English allies, the Percys of Northumberland, in 1403, but after 1405 his position gradually crumbled, while Henry's improved. He is rarely heard of after 1412, but seems to have lived until 1416 or later.

Owain Glyndwr

2 The Saxons, Normans and Plantagenets

Covering a period in history from the earliest Anglo-Saxon settlers to the last Plantagenet, Richard III, this section looks at the great rulers of the age. With such familiar names as Alfred the Great, Edward the Confessor, William the Conqueror and Henry V, this is a period rich in incident and intrigue.

Anglo-Saxon Kingdoms

The Germanic people from northern Germany and Scandinavia who settled lowland Britain in the fifth century AD were essentially tribal groups led by warrior-aristocrats under a chieftain or king. Supposedly descended from the god Wotan, this king was also a law-giver and was sanctified by rites which later developed into what we know as the Christian coronation, making the king also the champion of the Church.

The first English historian, the Venerable Bede (Baeda, c.673-735), described the Germanic settlers as Angles, Saxons and Jutes. He said that the Angles settled in the east, the Saxons in the south, and the Jutes in Kent. Archaeology suggests that this is roughly correct, although the situation was more complicated than Bede's simple description. Other groups, such as Franks, were certainly also involved.

England was at first divided into numerous little kingdoms, most of whose names and rulers are unknown. The main kingdoms that emerged were: Kent, Essex ('East Saxons'), Sussex ('South Saxons'), East Anglia, Lindsey, Bernicia, Deira, Mercia and Wessex ('West Saxons'). These were soon reduced to seven – the 'Anglo-Saxon

Hengist and Horsa established early Anglo-Saxon kingdoms

Heptarchy'. Lindsey, centred around Lincoln, was absorbed by its neighbours and disappeared. Bernicia and Deira combined to form Northumbria. In fact, the number of major kingdoms varied, and at different periods several of them in turn gained ascendancy over the others. Bede listed seven monarchs who held the title of 'Bretwalda', a high king acknowledged as superior by the other kings.

The area settled by the newcomers corresponds roughly to modern England, excluding Cornwall in the far south-west and, in the north, extending beyond the modern border, to the Forth. The British (Celtic) kingdom of Strathclyde included part of Cumbria. Frontiers were fluid, and the invasions of the Vikings caused almost total disruption of the Anglo-Saxon kingdoms in the ninth century.

Little or nothing is known of the early Anglo-Saxon monarchs beyond their names, and most dates are approximate.

Kent

Kent was the first of the Anglo-Saxon monarchies, and the first kingdom to achieve a degree of dominance over the others. It was also the first to be converted to Christianity, early in the seventh century. It appears to have maintained cross-Channel links and may have controlled trade with continental Europe. Its capital, Canterbury, became the headquarters of the English Church.

Vortigern, the southern high king, granted Hengist land in Kent

Hengist (died 488), was the founder of the Kentish kingdom.

Aesc, or **Oisc** (reigned c.488–512), gave his name, 'Oiscings' to the Kentish dynasty.

Octa (reigned c.512–40).

Eormenric (reigned c.540–60).

Ethelbert I, or **Aethelbert** (reigned c.560–616) Ethelbert I was acknowledged as Bretwalda by most of the other kingdoms. He married a Frankish, Christian princess, Bertha, and was himself converted to Christianity by St Augustine, the missionary appointed to convert the English by Pope Gregory the Great in 597. When he died he was buried in the new abbey church at Canterbury.

Eadbald (reigned 616-40), also married a Frankish princess, but temporarily abandoned Christianity.

Silver penny of Ethelbert

Earconbert (reigned 640–64).

Egbert (reigned 664–73).

Hlothere (reigned 673–85), succeeded his brother, Egbert. He was involved in dynastic contests and conflicts with neighbouring kingdoms, and died fighting the South Saxons on 6 February 685.

Eadric (reigned c.685–87), overthrew his predecessor and uncle with South Saxon help.

Oswini (reigned c.688–90).

Wihtred (reigned 690-725), was a powerful ruler, who threw off East Saxon influence and issued a code of laws.

Ethelbert II (reigned 725-62, jointly with his brother **Eadbert I** (725-48), half-brother Alric, and Eadbert's son **Eardwulf** (from c.747) was the father of King Egbert of Wessex.

Egbert II (reigned c.765-80).

Ealhmund (reigned c.784), when Kent was under Mercian control).

Eadbert II (reigned 796-98), was defeated and deposed by usurpers.

Cuthred (reigned 798-807), had one or two successors but, after the end of Mercian dominance (c.825), Kent came under the rule of the Kings of Wessex.

Essex

Although probably based on what is now London, Essex, which generally included the land of the Middle Saxons (Middlesex), never achieved much prominence among the Anglo-Saxon kingdoms. At one point Essex kings held some power in Kent, but they were submerged by the powerful Mercians in the eighth century and absorbed by Wessex early in the ninth century.

As in other early Anglo-Saxon kingdoms, many of the listed Kings of Essex were joint rulers.

Aescwine (reigned c.527-87), was reputedly the founder of the kingdom.

Sledda (reigned c.587-600).

Saebert (reigned c.600-16), adopted Christianity.

Sigeberht the Little (reigned c.617-50).

Sigeberht the Good (reigned c.650-60), restored Christianity after a lapse into paganism.

Swithhelm (reigned c.660-65).

Sighere (reigned c.665-83, jointly with his uncle Sebbe).

Sebbe (reigned c.665-95), was said to have abdicated in order to enter a monastery and was buried at St Paul's, London.

Sigheard (reigned c.695-c.708).

Swafred (reigned jointly with Sigheard, his brother), visited Rome in 709.

Offa (reigned c.709), was Sigheard's son and accompanied Swafred to Rome.

Saelred (reigned 709-46).

Swithred (reigned 746-c.758), was a grandson of Sigheard. His capital was at Colchester, where much of the Roman town survived, London being controlled by the Mercians.

Sigeric (reigned 758-98).

Sigered (reigned 798-825), was the last King of Essex.

Aelle, founder of Sussex

Sussex

Sussex and its kings, like those of Essex, are fairly obscure. The kingdom was said to have been founded by **Aelle**, who landed in 477. Bede named him as the first Bretwalda, although at that time there were no other kings of substance to make the title meaningful. His son **Cissa**, after whom the capital, Chichester, was named, succeeded him c.514. No other kings are known until the seventh century, when Sussex was dominated by other kingdoms, first by Mercia, and later by Wessex.

Ethelwah (reigned c.685), was converted to Christianity by St Wilfred, who founded the bishopric of Selsey. He was killed by Cadwalla of Wessex (see below).

Berthun (reigned c.685), perhaps a co-ruler, was killed in Kent.

Cadwalla (reigned c.686-88), was a usurper from Wessex.

Nothelm (reigned c.692).

Nunna (reigned c.710-25).

Aldwulf (reigned c.765).

Osmund (reigned c.765-70), was probably the last king before Sussex was absorbed by Mercia.

did you know?

It is likely that Ethelwah was installed as king by the powerful King Wulfhere of Mercia, following Ethelwah's conversion to Christianity. He was later killed in battle by the pagan West Saxon prince Cadwalla.

East Anglia

The kingdom of the East Angles included what became Norfolk, Suffolk and part of Cambridgeshire. It was relatively self-contained and prosperous. Its kings, most of them shadowy and some unknown, were called 'Wuffings', after the reputed founder of the kingdom. They retained their independence, though latterly under Northumbrian and Mercian dominance, until overrun by the Danes in the ninth century.

Wuffa (reigned c.571-78).

Tytila (reigned c.578-93).

Raedwald (reigned c.593-617), was said to have been a Christian who returned to paganism at the urging of his wife. He was named by Bede as Bretwalda of the Anglo-Saxons. He is the most likely person to have been the object of the ship burial at Sutton Hoo near Woodbridge in Suffolk, discovered in 1939. The treasure it contained, some of it from Byzantium, testifies to the wealth of the East Anglian kings.

Eorpwald (reigned c.617-27), son of Raedwald, was converted to Christianity by the pressure of King Edwin of Northumbria.

Siegeberht (reigned c.631-34), founded the bishopric of Dunwich, for St Felix, and a monastery. He abdicated in order to become a monk himself.

Siegeberht, the King-Monk

Ecgric (reigned c.634-35), was killed resisting King Penda of Mercia.

Anna (reigned c.633-54), though apparently installed as Penda's candidate for king, also died fighting the Mercians. He is remembered in legend as the father of several pious daughters.

Ethelhere, or **Aethelhere** (reigned 654), Anna's brother, was killed by Oswy of Northumbria.

Ethelwold, or **Aethelwald** (reigned c.654-63), was another of Anna's brothers.

Aldwulf (reigned c.663-713), the son of Ethelhere and a Northumbrian princess, also produced saintly daughters who became abbesses.

Aelfwald (reigned 713-49, while East Anglia was under Mercian domination).

Hun Beonna (reigned c.749).

Ethelbert (reigned 792), a saint and a martyr, was executed by Offa of Mercia, his father-in-law. He was later buried in St Ethelbert's Cathedral, Hereford.

Athelstan (reigned c.828-37), minted coins bearing his image.

Edmund (born c.840, reigned c.855-70), was the second and last East Anglian king to be canonized, after Ethelbert. He was killed by the Danes on 20 November 870 when he refused to renounce Christianity. Once England's patron saint (later superseded by St George), his remains were ultimately buried at Bury St Edmunds.

King Athelstan

weblink: http://en.wikipedia.org/wiki/Anglo-Saxon_Kings   Anglo-Saxon Kingdoms |

Northumbria

The kingdom of Northumbria (the name means 'land north of the Humber') was the first of the Anglo-Saxon kingdoms, after Kent, to gain national ascendancy. At its peak it included all the land between the Humber and the Forth and it was culturally advanced, producing, among other fine treasures, the Lindisfarne Gospels and was home to the first English historian, Bede, a monk at Jarrow.

Northumbria was created from the fusion of Bernicia, centred on Bamburgh and roughly equivalent to modern Northumberland, and Deira, centred on York. They were founded by **Ida** of Bernicia (reigned c.547-59). His son **Aelle** became King of Deira c.560-80.

Ethelfrith, or **Aethelfrith**, King of Bernicia (reigned c.593-616), was a younger son (possibly grandson) of Ida. He defeated the Picts and the Welsh, capturing Chester, and temporarily conquered Deira.

Edwin, King of Deira (reigned c.616-32), was a son of Aelle. He defeated and killed Ethelfrith in alliance with King Raedwald of East Anglia, regaining Deira. He also conquered several smaller kingdoms, including Lindsey, and was acknowledged as Bretwalda. He married Ethelburga, daughter of Ethelbert of Kent, and became a Christian under her influence (627). He was killed on 13 October 633, fighting against Penda of Mercia and Cadwallon of Gwynedd, at Hatfield Chase.

Eanfrith, King of Bernicia (reigned 633-34), the son of Ethelfrith, he briefly regained Bernicia before dying in battle.

Oswald (born c.605, reigned c.634-42) was the son of Ethelfrith and brother of Eanfrith. He reunited Deira and Bernicia and succeeded Edwin as Bretwalda. In exile under Edwin, he apparently visited Iona, which inspired him with religious passion. He defeated Cadwallon of Gwynedd in 634, uniting Bernicia and Deira. In 635 he also asked for a bishop from the Scots, receiving Aidan, to whom he gave the holy isle of Lindisfarne. He was killed in battle against Penda of Mercia.

Oswy (born c.602, reigned 642-70), brother or half-brother of Oswald, was the last Bretwalda listed by Bede and the last notable Northumbrian king. He threw off Mercian domination and turned the tables by temporarily annexing Mercia and introducing Christianity. In the north he defeated the Britons of Strathclyde, the Scots and the Picts. As his second wife he married Eanfled, daughter of Edwin and Ethelburga. He died on 15 February 670.

Egrith (reigned 670-85), was the son of Oswy and Eanfled. His excursions across the Humber and north of the Forth were repulsed by, respectively, the Mercians and the Picts, who killed him at Nechtansmere, near Forfar.

Aldfrith (reigned 685-704), illegitimate son of Oswy, was a great patron of scholarship and the arts.

Osred I (reigned 704-16).

Coenred (reigned 716-18).

Osric (reigned 718-29).

Ceolwulf (reigned 729-37), was the 'most glorious king', to whom Bede (see above) dedicated his *Ecclesiastical History of the English People*. He was deposed in 736, restored, but abdicated in 737 and ended his life as a monk at Lindisfarne.

Eadbert (reigned 737-58), invaded the territory of the Picts and the British of Strathclyde, capturing Dumbarton in 756, but eventually followed his predecessor into a monastery.

Oswulf (reigned 758-59).

Ethelwald Moll (reigned 759-65), defeated a rebellion but was later forced to abdicate.

Alchred (reigned 765-74).

Ethelred I (reigned 774-96 with interruptions), was overthrown in 778, regained his crown in 790, and was killed at Corbridge in 796.

Elfwald I (reigned 778-88), replaced the deposed Ethelred, but was murdered in 788.

Osred II (reigned 788-90), was killed by Ethelred, who then regained the Crown.

Osbald (reigned 796). His reign is said to have lasted less than a month.

Eardwulf (reigned 796-809, with interruptions).

Elfwald II (reigned c.808).

Eanred (reigned 809-41) paid homage to Egbert of Wessex in 827.

Ethelred II (reigned 841-48).

Osberht (reigned 848-63, died 866).

Ella, or **Aelle** (reigned 863-67), briefly regained York from the Norsemen in 866, but was killed in battle the following year. His successors were subject to the Norsemen, with restricted authority.

Egbert I (reigned 867-72).

Ricsig (reigned 872-76).

Egbert II (reigned 876-78).

Mercia

The original kingdom of Mercia occupied roughly what is now the West Midlands. The name refers to 'marches' (border areas), presumably alluding to the proximity of Wales, though the first centre of the kingdom appears to have been on the upper Trent. In Mercia's age of greatness, in the seventh and eighth centuries, its kings ruled all England, except East Anglia, from the Humber to south of the Thames, including London. Its prosperity was largely based on the control of trade, which provided its kings, for virtually the first time, with a reliable and substantial source of revenue.

King Offa of Mercia

Creoda (reigned c.585-93), is the first documented King of Mercia, supposedly descended from a legendary founder named **Icel**.

Pybba (reigned c.592-606).

Ceorl (reigned c.606-26). His daughter married the Northumbrian king, Edwin, who held authority over him.

Penda (reigned 632 (?626)-55) was a renowned warrior, and a pagan, who was involved in a long contest with Northumbria (and was therefore roughly treated by Bede). He defeated the men of Wessex at Cirencester in 628, extending his kingdom south of the Severn. In alliance with Cadwallon of Gwynedd he defeated and killed Edwin of Northumbria in 633, and his successor, Oswald, in 641, attacking, but failing to capture, the Bernician stronghold of Bamburgh, and temporarily ending Mercian subservience to Northumbria. He was finally killed by Oswy in 654 or 655. His conquests were divided among his sons, who became Christians, under Northumbrian suzerainty.

Wulfhere (reigned 657-75) was a younger son of Penda. He threw off Northumbrian supremacy, and invaded Wessex, capturing the Isle of Wight, but lost Lindsey to Egfrith of Northumbria.

Ethelred, or **Aethelred** (reigned 675-704), another son of Penda (see left), regained Lindsey before retiring to a monastery.

Coenred (reigned 704-9), son of Wulfhere, also forsook the rough life of kingship and made a pilgrimage to Rome.

Coelred (reigned 709-16).

Ethelbald, or **Aethelbald** (reigned 716-57), was the scion of a distant branch of the royal house. During his long reign he restored Mercian domination of middle England, and added territory conquered from Wessex. He was murdered by his own people at Seckington, Warwickshire, and was buried at Repton Abbey.

Beonred (reigned 757).

Offa (reigned 757-96), was descended from a brother of Penda. He was the most successful Anglo-Saxon king before Alfred. He reduced the authority of sub-kings and controlled almost all England south of the Humber. He built the earthworks known as Offa's Dyke on the western frontier, to exclude raids by the Welsh and facilitate his own raids into Wales. He established a business relationship with Charlemagne and issued an elaborate silver coinage. Some coins bear the head of his queen, Cynethryth, a practice of the Roman emperors with whom he perhaps identified. He began the practice of annointing his son as king in his own lifetime, to end succession conflicts.

Egfrith (reigned 796), Offa's son, was co-king from 787. He outlived his father by only five months.

Coenwulf (reigned 796-821), belonged to a different branch of the royal house from Offa.

Ceolwulf I (reigned 821-23), a brother of Coenwulf, was soon deposed.

Beornwulf (reigned 825), was defeated by Egbert of Wessex and killed by the East

Angles. His brief reign marks the end of Mercian ascendancy.

Ludeca (reigned 827).

Wiglaf (reigned 827-40), was deposed by Egbert of Wessex in 829 but subsequently regained the kingship. He was buried at Repton Abbey.

Beorhtwulf, or **Berthwulf** (reigned 840-52).

Burgred (reigned 852-74), seems to have been dependent on Wessex, marrying Ethelswith, daughter of Ethelwulf of Wessex, whom he assisted in his war in North Wales and with whom he co-operated against the Vikings. The Danish host, which was encroaching on Mercia, eventually deposed Burgred, who died in Rome.

Ceolwulf II (reigned 874-c.880) was installed by the Danes as king of the unoccupied portion of Mercia, but later deposed.

Wessex

Founded c.494, Wessex originally occupied the southern, central counties of England. It replaced Mercia as the dominant Anglo-Saxon kingdom in the early ninth century, a time when Danish raids were increasing. Wessex alone survived the Scandinavian invasions. It gradually absorbed the other kingdoms, and the Kings of Wessex thus became Kings of England.

Cerdic (reigned 519-34), the first documented King of Wessex (and ancestor of the present queen), landed in Hampshire c.494, defeated the local British king and later added the Isle of Wight to his conquests.

Cynric (reigned 534-60), son of Cerdic, expanded the kingdom into Wiltshire.

Ceawlin (reigned 560-91/92), son of Cynric, continued the expansion, his authority extending north of the Thames valley. He held temporary ascendancy over all the southern Anglo-Saxon kings. He was listed by Bede as the second Bretwalda, though was eventually driven from the throne, dying soon afterwards.

Ceorl (reigned 591-97).

Ceolwulf (reigned 597-611).

Cynegils (reigned 611-43), was the first Christian King of Wessex. An attempt to murder King Edwin of Northumbria provoked invasion, and there were also clashes with Penda of Mercia, leading to the loss of the Severn valley sub-kingdom of Hwicce.

Cenwalh (reigned 643-72, with interruptions), son of Cynegils, married and then discarded Penda's sister. The Mercian revenge resulted in loss of territory, including much of Somerset, Hampshire and the Isle of Wight. Cenwalh fled to East Anglia, but subsequently regained his kingdom and founded the cathedral at Winchester (648), where he was buried.

did you know?

Anglo-Saxon kingdoms were belligerent and quarrelsome, constantly fighting for political, territorial and religious power. While some kings Christianized their populations, others still worshipped pagan gods, and gave offerings of human heads after battle.

Seaxburgh (reigned c.673), widow of Cenwalh, apparently reigned briefly in her own right, the only known Anglo-Saxon queen regnant.

Cenfus (reigned c.674).

Aescwine (reigned 674-76).

Centwine (reigned 676-85).

Cadwalla, or **Ceadwalla** (reigned 685-88), began the restoration of Wessex, retaking the Isle of Wight, before abdicating and going to Rome, where he died on 20 April 688.

Ine (reigned 688-726), completed the reconstruction of the kingdom, greatly extending its frontiers to the west, defeating the Britons of Cornwall, as well as the King of Sussex. He was credited with founding the port of Southampton before he abdicated and died on his way to Rome.

Ethelheard, or **Aethelheard** (reigned 726-40), ruled during Mercian predominance.

Cuthred (reigned 740-56).

Sigeberht (reigned 756-57), fell out with his nobles, after killing one of their fellows, and was expelled by his successor, though he held on to Hampshire for a time, before being murdered.

Cynewulf (reigned 757-86), was murdered by Sigeberht's brother.

Berhtric (reigned 786-802), married the daughter of his dominant neighbour, Offa of Mercia. Viking raids on Wessex began during Berhtric's reign.

Egbert (reigned 802-39), was the first of a line of powerful Wessex kings. He spent some early years in exile at the court of Charlemagne and was sub-king of Kent before succeeding his cousin, Berhtric. He married Redburga, a Frankish princess. His defeat of Beornwulf of Mercia at the Battle of Ellandune, near Swindon, in 825 marks the replacement of Mercia by Wessex as the leading kingdom. By the end of his reign, Egbert dominated all England south of the Humber. The lesser kingdoms were finally extinguished, the Cornishmen were defeated, and Danish raiders repulsed. Egbert issued a silver coinage, the earliest known from Wessex.

Ethelwulf (reigned 839-58), was crowned at Kingston-upon-Thames. Son of Egbert, he ruled jointly with his father and his younger brother. He married Osburga, and four of their sons, including Alfred, became Kings of Wessex. Ethelwulf was involved in incessant wars against the Danes, winning a notable victory at Ockley in Surrey (851). His gold ring is now preserved in the British Museum.

Ethelbald (reigned 858-60), son of Ethelwulf, married his father's widow, Judith, a Frankish princess, but the marriage was annulled. There were no children.

Ethelbert, or **Aethelbert** (reigned 860-65), previously sub-king of Kent, was unable to prevent the Danes sacking Winchester in 860. He was buried at Sherborne Abbey.

Ethelred, or **Aethelred** (reigned 865-71), was ruling at the time of the full-scale invasion by the Danes' 'Great Army'. In 871, when the all-conquering Danes turned against Wessex, Ethelred, with his younger brother Alfred, fought a succession of battles, receiving mortal wounds at Merton, Oxfordshire. He was buried at Wimborne Minster.

The Vikings and the House of Wessex

The Vikings of Scandinavia made a name for themselves in England and Europe as raiders and marauders capable of all sorts of hideous atrocities. In time though, they came to England in another, less ferocious guise: as settlers aiming to make new lives for themselves.

The first Viking raid was recorded by the *Anglo-Saxon Chronicle* in 789. In the next few years northern coasts were raided and the great religious centres of Lindisfarne and Jarrow were sacked. By the 830s the raids of the pagan Vikings – in England mostly Danes – occurred almost every year.

In the 850s the raids became more substantial. The 'Great Army' that invaded East Anglia under Halfdan and Ivarr the Boneless in 865 was bent on conquest and settlement. Their most significant settlement was in what was then Northumbria. Within three years it had conquered northern and eastern England. By 874 only one English kingdom remained independent: Wessex.

By a mixture of good luck and good leadership, Alfred of Wessex checked the Danes' advance and preserved Wessex's independence. His successors gradually drove the Danes out and, in the process, became kings of a single country (though it was not yet called 'England').

The Danish leader, Guthrum, made peace with Alfred after Alfred's victory at Edington in May 878. He was baptized a Christian, a symbol of political agreement, and forced to leave Wessex.

By the agreement of 878, made at Wedmore, Somerset, the Danes kept to the region north-west of a line from London to Chester, which became known as the 'Danelaw'.

Viking sea raiders

Saxon Kings of England

England became united under the royal house of Wessex during the ninth and tenth centuries. Several monarchs played a part in this, but Athelstan, son of Edward the Elder and grandson of Alfred the Great, is generally regarded as the first king of a whole, united England.

Alfred, 'the Great'

must know

Born: Wantage, Berkshire, c.849
Parents: Ethelwulf of Wessex and Osburga
Ascended the throne: 23 April 871
Coronation: Possibly Kingston-upon-Thames, 871
Married: Ethelswitha, a Mercian princess
Children: Three daughters and three sons, including Ethelfleda, or Aethelfleda, of Mercia and King Edward the Elder
Died: c.26 October 899
Buried: Newminster Abbey, Winchester

Alfred the Great is probably best known for his defence against the Vikings and his encouragement of learning and education. However, his worthiness as a ruler was seen in other areas too. Almost as soon as he came to the throne, he set about repairing and fortifying his kingdom in Wessex. His achievements were unsurpassed for their time and he truly laid down the foundations for a united English realm.

The threat of Viking invasion was ever-present: Alfred's major occupation when he first came to the throne was that of fending off the marauders. After fierce fighting in 871, the Danes temporarily withdrew from Wessex, but returned in force in 878. Alfred fled to the Somerset levels, then undrained. He emerged from hiding to defeat the Danes at Edington in Wiltshire (May 878). Alfred laid the basis for the unification of England, building a system of fortified towns in Wessex and creating a substantial navy. He devised new laws, based on custom and consultation, and encouraged cultural developments, personally translating several books from Latin.

Edward, 'the Elder'

must know

Born: c.871
Parents: King Alfred and Ethelswitha
Ascended the throne: c.26 Oct 899
Coronation: Kingston-upon-Thames, 31 May/8 June 900
Married: (1) Egwina, (2) Elfleda, daughter of a nobleman, (3) Edgiva, daughter of a Kentish noble
Children: With (1), two sons including King Athelstan and (St) Edith; with (2), two sons and eight daughters; with (3), two sons, Edmund I and Edred, and two daughters
Died: Farndon-on-Dee, 17 July 924
Buried: Winchester Cathedral

The creation of the Danelaw had been a compromise made by Edward's father, ceding approximately half of England, in the north and east, to Danish rule to earn a period of relative calm for war-torn England. Edward was determined to reconquer the Danelaw. He captured the Danish 'Five Boroughs' (now the East Midlands and Lincolnshire), and built more forts in the sub-kingdom of Mercia, which he inherited on the death of his sister Ethelflaed in 918.

Several of his daughters married continental rulers.

Edward, 'the Elder'

Athelstan

must know

Born: c.895
Parents: Edward the Elder and Egwina
Ascended the throne: 17 July 924
Coronation: Kingston-upon-Thames, 4 September 925
Authority: King of England
Married: Unmarried
Died: Gloucester, 27 October 939
Buried: Malmesbury Abbey

did you know?

The Battle of Brunanburh was one of King Athelstan's greatest triumphs. Olaf led a large Viking army from Ireland. The Vikings, however, although joined by the Scots, were unable to overcome King Athelstan. He is regarded by many historians as the first English king, and was crowned at Kingston-upon-Thames in AD 925

Athelstan was a remarkable character, with a natural authority recognised and conceded by even the fiercest of his rivals.

He was sent away from his father's court at Winchester – probably because he was illegitimate – and brought up by his aunt, Athelflaed, at Gloucester, in Mercia. Consequently the Mercians came to regard him as one of their own, making it easier for them to accept him as their king. Wessex, where his irregular birth may have worked against him, took a little longer to follow suit.

The crucial date for the ascendancy of Athelstan is perhaps 937, when he defeated the Scots and Danes at the Battle of Brunanburh. He was recognized as overlord in Cornwall, Scotland and Wales, although that meant little in practical terms. Like his grandfather, he was remembered also as a law-giver and tactful governor.

Athelstan maintained extensive European connections through the marriages of his numerous sisters.

Malmesbury Abbey

Edmund I, 'the Magnificent'

must know

Born: c.921
Parents: Edward the Elder and Edgiva of Kent
Ascended the throne: 27 October 939
Coronation: Kingston-upon-Thames, 29 November 939
Authority: King of England
Married: (1) (St) Elgiva, (2) Ethelfleda, daughter of the Ealdorman of Wiltshire
Children: With (1), two sons, the future Kings Edwy and Edgar, and one daughter
Died: Pucklechurch, Gloucestershire, 26 May 946
Buried: Glastonbury Abbey

Another formidable warrior, Edmund I fought with his predecessor and half-brother, Edward, at Brunanburh. He retrieved part of Northumbria conquered by the Norse King of York, Olaf Guthfrithson, and defeated the Britons of Strathclyde, which he turned over to the King of Scots. By 944 his authority was acknowledged throughout England.

Edred

must know

Born: c.923
Parents: Edward the Elder and Edgiva of Kent
Ascended the throne: 26 May 946
Coronation: Kingston-upon-Thames, 16 August 946
Authority: King of England
Died: Frome, Somerset, 23 November 955
Buried: Winchester Cathedral

did you know?

Despite suffering from an unidentified illness which eventually killed him, Edred succeeded to the English throne in AD 946 after the unexpected murder of his brother, Edmund. The people of the north finally recognized him as their monarch in AD 954, and the Norse monarchy of York never returned.

In spite of health problems, Edred proved an effective war leader, expelling the Norsemen who had reclaimed York by defeating their leader, Eric Bloodaxe (died 954), and re-enforcing royal authority in Northumbria.

Edwy, 'the Fair'

Born: c.941
Parents: Edmund I and (St) Elgiva
Ascended the throne: 23 November 955
Coronation: Kingston-upon-Thames, c.26 January 956
Authority: King of England
Married: Elgiva (Elgifu), his stepsister
Died: Gloucester, 1 October 959
Buried: Winchester Cathedral

Edwy was just a boy when chosen to succeed his uncle, Edred. He soon dismissed Dunstan, the Abbot of Glastonbury, who legend has it offended the sovereign during his annointing ceremony. Dunstan was banished in 956, but later became Archbishop of Canterbury under Edgar, Edwy's brother and successor.

Edwy antagonized the Archbishop of Canterbury, Oda, and the influential Abbot of Glastonbury, (St) Dunstan, by his secret marriage to his stepmother's daughter. According to the *Anglo-Saxon Chronicle*, the marriage was later annulled. Elgiva died in Gloucester in suspicious circumstances in September 959, and the king died soon afterwards.

Edgar

Born: c.943
Parents: Edmund I and (St) Elgiva
Ascended the throne: 1 October 959
Coronation: Bath Abbey, 11 May 973
Authority: 'King of the English and of the other people living within Britain'
Married: (1) Ethelfleda, daughter of an ealdorman, (2) Elfrida, daughter of the ealdorman of Devon
Children: With (1), one son, the future King Edward the Martyr; with (2), two sons, Edmund and Ethelred II; one illegitimate daughter, (St) Edith, or Eadgyth
Died: Winchester, 8 July 975
Buried: Glastonbury Abbey

Edgar was sub-king of Mercia and Northumbria from 957 before succeeding as King of England. He favoured (St) Dunstan who, as Archbishop of Canterbury (961-88), had a powerful influence on Edgar during his largely peaceful reign. He was acknowledged as overlord by the King of Scots, to whom he surrendered Lothian.

Edgar's late coronation followed rites devised by (St) Dunstan, which form the basis of the coronation ceremony today (previous kings had been consecrated rather than crowned). Elfrida was crowned with him, and this was another innovation.

(St) Edward II, 'the Martyr'

must know

Born: c.963
Parents: King Edgar and Ethelfleda
Ascended the throne: 8 July 975
Coronation: Kingston-upon-Thames, 975
Authority: King of England
Died: Corfe Castle, Dorset, 18 March 978
Buried: Wareham, Dorset; in 980 translated to Shaftesbury Abbey

did you know?

Edward 'the Martyr' had a short and tragic reign. He was murdered at 16 by members of his stepmother's household, who stabbed him to death as he dismounted his horse. When miracles appeared to happen by his grave, his successor, Ethelred, proclaimed him a saint and martyr.

Edward, though influenced by (St) Dunstan, failed to prevent an anti-monastic reaction during his reign. His stepmother, Elfrida of Devon, had some support for her belief that her own son, Ethelred, ought to be king. On a visit to them at Corfe, the young King Edward was ambushed and murdered. (The final resting place of his alleged remains, unearthed by archaeologists in 1931, caused a dispute. At one time they were in the custody of the Midland Bank, Croydon.)

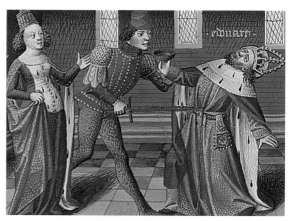

Edward being murdered at Corfe Castle

Ethelred II, 'the Unready'

must know

Born: c.968

Parents: King Edgar and Elfrida

Ascended the throne: 18 March 978

Coronation: Kingston-upon-Thames, April 978

Authority: King of England

Married: (1) Elfleda, or Elgiva, daughter of an ealdorman, (2) Emma, daughter of the Duke of Normandy

Children: With (1), eight sons, including Edmund II, and five daughters;with (2), two sons, including Edward the Confessor, and one daughter

Died: London, 23 April 1016

Buried: St Paul's Cathedral

Called *unraed*, or 'the Redeless', meaning 'uncounselled' rather than 'unready', Ethelred failed the first test of medieval kingship – success as a war leader. He could not prevent new Viking attacks and was forced to buy off King Olaf Tryggvesson of Norway and King Sweyn of Denmark when, provoked by Ethelred's massacre of Anglo-Danes, they sailed up the Thames to threaten London in 994. Famine and an epidemic among the cattle exacerbated his woes. In 1013 Sweyn forced Ethelred from the throne and into exile in Normandy. Ethelred returned, however the following year, after Sweyn's early death, to rule a short while longer.

Ethelred II, 'the Unready'

Danish Kings

Between 875 and 954 a number of Danish and Norse kings preserved a semi-independent enclave in the Scandinavian kingdom of York. From 994 a more formidable Danish assault was launched against England, resulting in a brief dynasty of Danish kings.

Danish raiders attacking the English Coast

Sweyn, 'Forkbeard'

must know

Born: c.990
Parents: King Harold Bluetooth of Denmark; mother uncertain
Ascended the throne: Denmark 986, England 1013
Coronation: Not crowned in England
Authority: King of Denmark, Norway and England
Married: (1) Gunhilda, probably a Polish princess, (2) Sigrid, former wife of the King of Sweden
Children: With (1), two sons, including Canute; with (2), one daughter; four other daughters with either (1) or (2)
Died: Gainsborough, Lincolnshire, 3 February 1014
Buried: London; later removed to Roskilde Cathedral, Denmark

A formidable warrior, Sweyn seized the Danish Crown from his father and created an empire centred on the North Sea. After several earlier attacks, he drove out Ethelred in the autumn of 1013 and was accepted as king. A few weeks later, however, he died as a result of a fall from his horse.

Sweyn dreamt of his death by drowning

Edmund II, 'Ironside'

must know

Born: c.990
Parents: Ethelred II and Elfleda
Ascended the throne: 23 April 1016
Coronation: St Paul's Cathedral, London, c.25 April 1016
Authority: King of England
Married: Edith (or Eagwyth), widow of an East Anglian thegn
Children: Two sons, including Edward the Atheling
Died: London (or possibly Oxford), 30 November 1016
Buried: Glastonbury Abbey

did you know?

Edmund 'Ironside' was a courageous prince who, during a short reign, proved himself a brave monarch. Unlike his father Ethelred, who earned himself the telling moniker 'the Unready', Edmund was decisive and determined as well as being an inspirational leader. He was seriously wounded during the battle of Ashingdon and died after just seven months' reign.

Edmund grew up during a period when England's fortunes were at a low ebb because of repeated Viking incursions.His campaign against his Scandinavian enemy, Canute, resulted in the division of the kingdom.

Perceptive even in his youth, Edmund recognised the flaws in his father's policy of buying off the Vikings, and as a prince encouraged the country to stand up against them. A fine warrior and a determined leader, he was the opposite of his father, Ethelred the Unready. His valour earned him the epithet 'Ironside'.

In 1014 Canute had left England to stake his claim for the throne of Denmark. When he returned in 1015, Ethelred's army was not prepared. Only Edmund had the presence of mind to turn and face this resurfaced challenge to his father's throne. He marched southwards to meet Canute, intending to combine his forces with those of Edric of Mercia, but Edric turned traitor and Edmund's defence failed. The final battle took place at Ashingdon in Essex. Edmund's defeat there was less to do with his war-weary forces (both sides were suffering from the relentless campaign) and more the result of Edric's treachery yet again. Having been forgiven for his earlier acts, Edric and his forces began the battle on Edmund's side but, once again, switched allegiance.

When Ethelred died in 1016, London and the Witan members there chose Edmund as king, but the Witan in Southampton opted for Canute. At Olney, Edmund and Canute agreed to partition England, though the longer lived would succeed to the whole. However, a few weeks later Edmund died after a reign of only seven months and his infant sons fled Canute's rule to settle in Hungary.

Canute, or Cnut

must know

Born: c.995
Parents: King Sweyn and Gunhildaof Poland
Ascended the throne: 30 November 1016
Coronation: Possibly St Paul's Cathedral, London, c.1017
Authority: King of England, Denmark (from 1019) and Norway (from 1028)
Married: (1) Elgiva, daughter of the Ealdorman of Deira, never consecrated;
(2) Emma of Normandy, widow of Ethelred II
Children: With (1), two sons, Harold Harefoot and Sweyn; with (2), one son, Harthacanute,
and two daughters; several illegitimate children
Died: Shaftesbury, 12 November 1035
Buried: Winchester Cathedral

Canute came to England in 1013, when his father invaded the country in response to the murder, by Saxons, of a group of Dqanish settlers. At that time and for many years before, possesssion of England had been hotly disputed between the Saxons and the Vikings, both of them originally invaders from Europe.

When Edmund Ironside died, Canute succeeded to the whole English kingdom. He spent most of his time in England though Denmark occupied him increasingly from the 1020s. While ruthless in establishing his position, and maintaining a Danish standing army, he afterwards earned respect by pursuing statesmanlike policies, founding monasteries and encouraging trade. He employed Englishmen as well as Danes.

Legend relates how Canute mocked his courtiers' obsequiousness by disproving their assertion that the tide would retreat at his command.

King Canute

Harold I, 'Harefoot'

must know

Born: c.1016
Parents: King Canute and Elgiva
Ascended the throne: 12 November 1035
Coronation: Oxford, 1037
Authority: King of England
Married: Elgiva
Children: One son
Died: Oxford, 17 March 1040
Buried: Possibly Westminster Abbey; disinterred by his successor

Harold I, 'Harefoot'

Harold I ruled England as regent for his younger half-brother, Harthacanute, King of Denmark, but in 1037 claimed the Crown in his own right. This caused a breach with the queen dowager, Emma, who went into exile in Flanders.

Harthacanute, or Hardicanute

must know

Born: c.1018
Parents: King Canute and Emma of Normandy
Ascended the throne: 12 November 1035
Coronation: Possibly Canterbury Cathedral, June 1040
Authority: King of Denmark and England
Died: Lambeth, London, 8 June 1042
Buried: Winchester Cathedral

did you know?

Harthacanute was about two years younger than Harold I but his legitimate birth placed him in a better position to become king. He was the accepted heir to Canute's throne and Harold had to wait until Harthacanute was absent before he could make his own bid for power. His popularity was short-lived, however.

Harthacanute's reign was brief but violent. He arrived with a large fleet to claim the Crown on the death of Harold Harefoot, whose body he had thrown into a marsh. Excessive taxes made him unpopular. He burned Worcester after the murder of royal tax-collectors. He died of 'a horrible convulsion' while attending a wedding.

Edward, 'the Confessor'

Although Edward was half-brother to Harthacanute, his accession restored the royal house of Wessex to the English throne. He was, though, more Norman than English, having spent 28 years of Danish rule at the Norman court. Norman influence in England expanded greatly during his reign. It was resisted by the English, especially by the powerful Earl Godwine (died 1053) and his son Harold, virtual ruler in Edward's later years.

Powerful families close to the throne were a serious problem for medieval kings. Godwine, Earl of Wessex, buttressed his power base by carefully ensuring that his children were placed in advantageous positions: two sons were made earls, and his daughter was married to Edward. One of Godwine's sons eventually succeeded the childless Edward as King Harold II.

Pious to a fault, Edward was canonized a century after his death. On religious grounds, he declined to consummate his marriage, and lack of a direct heir promised conflict over the succession. Edward allegedly promised the Crown to Duke William of Normandy, but on his deathbed he was said to have named Harold Godwineson as his successor.

Edward, 'the Confessor'

Harold II

must know

Born: c.1020

Parents: Earl Godwine of Wessex and Gytha, a Danish princess

Ascended the throne: 5 Jan 1066

Coronation: Westminster Abbey, 6 Jan 1066

Authority: King of England

Married: Ealgith, daughter of the Earl of Mercia and widow of Gruffydd ap Llywelyn

Children: One or two sons; six or seven illegitimate children with Edith 'Swan-neck'

Died: Senlac, Sussex, 14 October 1066

Buried: Pevensey Bay, later allegedly removed to Waltham Abbey by Edith Swan-neck

The Norman Conquest, as depicted in the Bayeux Tapestry

In the very first week of 1066, the death of Edward created a succession struggle. Harold, Earl of Wessex, was selected but three other rival claims would soon be pressed. The man with the best hereditary claim to the Crown upon Edward the Confessor's death was Edgar the Atheling, grandson of Edmund Ironside (and brother-in-law of Malcolm III, King of Scots). He stood little chance, however. Harold was the man in possession, he had a proven record, and he was unanimously approved by the Witan.

Other claimants proved more formidable. The first, King Harold Hardrada of Norway, supported by King Harold's brother, Tostig, invaded Northumbria but was defeated and killed by Harold at Stamford Bridge near York on 25 September 1066.

Three days later another claimant, Duke William of Normandy, landed in Sussex. He maintained that Harold had recognized him as heir to the Crown when shipwrecked in Normandy in 1064. Whatever the truth of this claim, William prepared to do battle with the newly crowned King Harold II. Marching rapidly south from the scene of his victory just days earlier, Harold confronted William near Hastings, and was killed in battle.

The Norman Conquest

Descended from Viking settlers, the Normans were the most formidable people in eleventh-century Europe. They founded a kingdom in Sicily as well as in England. The Duke of Normandy was a more substantial figure than his nominal overlord, the King of France.

William the Conqueror was only seven years old when he inherited the title of Duke of Normandy, and the next decade in his life was full of menace. All three of the boy's leading protectors were murdered, as potential usurpers sought to overthrow William and his supporters. However, one friendly face in the duchy was an exiled noble, who was the young duke's distant cousin. This exile was the son of Ethelred the Unready; he would later rule England as Edward the Confessor.

The Norman Conquest brought great changes to England, although recent historians point out, first, that this was a period of great change all over Europe and, second, that surviving historical documents are far more numerous for this period than for before, which may make long-established arrangements appear as new.

There were great cultural changes. The Normans made French, rather than English, the everyday language of the élite. The developments most obvious today were architectural. The Normans were great builders: many of their castles and churches still stand. The style, known as Romanesque on the continent, is in Britain called Norman.

The Normans were well-organized. It is now generally believed that they did not introduce feudalism, in which men held land in exchange for service, but, rather, made it more pervasive and coherent.

The Norman kings were continental rulers. Accordingly, England was drawn closely into European affairs. From 1066 until the fifteenth century, the King of England was also a French prince (for part of that time he claimed to be King of France). European dynastic conflicts became a dominant concern of government.

King Harold had hoped to take the invading Normans by surprise, at the cost of fielding a small and exhausted army, which had marched 240 miles in 13 days. In this time the Norman soldiers had been familiarising themselves with the lie of the land, while Harold's men were enduring the strains of battle at far-off Stamford Bridge. Although the English forces had the advantage of holding a hill-top, a Norman feint lured them from their position and they were defeated.

The Normans advanced on London, ravaging Kent and burning Southwark. Opposition faded, and William was accepted as king, but five years passed, with frequent rebellions, before Norman rule was secure.

The Normans entrenched their rule by building castles to control towns and other strategic points. Gradually, the big English landholders were replaced by Normans. Eventually, almost the whole ruling class, not merely the dynasty, was changed.

Death of Harold

The Norman Conquest is recorded in the 72 scenes of the Bayeux Tapestry. The scene of Harold's death seems to show that he was killed by an arrow in the eye. Closer examination shows that this is a different figure. Harold was killed by a sword.

With the defeat of Harold at the Battle of Hastings, a reign of just nine months dramatically ended. More significantly, a single day's fighting sounded the death knell not just for Harold, but also for the Anglo-Saxon line of English and Danish kings.

William's coronation

It was said that cheers rang out in Westminster Abbey as William was crowned on Christmas Day 1066. This made the guards outside think a riot had broken out, and they set fire to the surrounding buildings. The consecration went on inside in spite of the flames, though even William, legend has it, was trembling like a leaf.

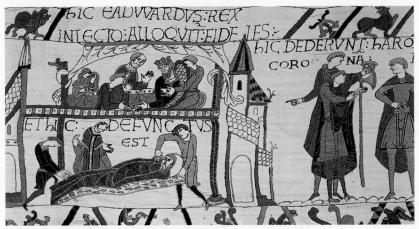

The Bayeux Tapestry is over 70 m (230 ft) long

William I, 'the Conqueror'

must know

Born: Falaise, 1027 or 1028
Parents: Robert, Duke of Normandy and Herleva, a tanner's daughter
Ascended the throne: 25 December 1066
Coronation: Westminster Abbey, 25 December 1066
Authority: King of England and Duke of Normandy
Married: Matilda, daughter of the Count of Flanders, c.1050
Children: Four sons, including the future kings, William II and Henry I, and six daughters
Died: 9 September 1087
Buried: St Stephen's Abbey, Caen, Normandy

Known as William the Bastard, he succeeded his father, who had no legitimate heir, as Duke of Normandy in 1035. He became Count of Maine by conquest in 1063. He claimed the English Crown, formally, by right of inheritance: he was first cousin once removed to Edward the Confessor, and his wife was directly descended from Alfred the Great. More realistically, he also claimed it by conquest.

William suppressed a widespread rebellion in the north in person (1069). Afterwards he ravaged the country so severely it took generations to recover.

♕ William was only seven years old when he became Duke of Normandy.
♕ William ordered a detailed inventory of his new kingdom, Domesday Book (1086), an example of Norman efficiency.
♕ William died, campaigning in France, after the pommel of his saddle struck him in the stomach.

William receives allegiance

WILLIAM ᛫CONQVEROR

William I, 'the Conqueror'

William II, 'Rufus'

William, named 'Rufus' because of his ruddy complexion and red hair, was the third son of William I. The eldest, Robert Curthose, succeeded as Duke of Normandy; the second, Richard, had predeceased his father. Rufus crushed revolts of Anglo-Norman vassals in support of Robert and later gained control of Normandy – which was vital in order to end the dual loyalty of his chief vassals – when Robert went on crusade. He invaded Scotland, killing Malcolm III, and forced obeisance among the Scots and Welsh.

Divine disapproval

Rufus incurred the hostility of the Church, keeping bishoprics and abbeys vacant to milk their revenue and driving the reforming Archbishop of Canterbury, Anselm, into exile. Since chronicles were written by monks, Rufus acquired a poor reputation.

An effete court

The chronicler William of Malmesbury hinted that Rufus was homosexual, surrounded by young men who 'rival young women in delicacy'. Rufus seems never to have shown interest in the latter.

Like his brother Richard (gored by a stag), Rufus died in the New Forest. Following their conquest of England, one of the Normans' priorities was to section off areas of forest solely for use by the king and his courtiers, for the pursuit of one of their favourite sports: hunting. He was shot while hunting by a knight named Walter Tyrel. Tyrel said it was an accident. There were no other witnesses. The Rufus Stone in the New Forest marks the alleged site of his death.

William II, 'Rufus'

Henry I

must know

Born: Selby, Yorkshire, c.September 1068
Parents: William I and Matilda of Flanders
Ascended the throne: 3 August 1100
Coronation: Westminster Abbey, 5 August 1100
Authority: King of England and Duke of Normandy (from 1106)
Married: (1) Matilda (born Edith), daughter of Malcolm III, King of Scots, and (St) Margaret, (2) Adelicia,or Adelaide, daughter of Geoffrey VII, Count of Louvain
Children: With (1), two sons and two daughters; others illegitimate children
Died: St Denis le Fermont, near Rouen, 2 December 1135
Buried: Reading Abbey

English-born and well-educated (probably, as a younger son, with an ecclesiastical career in mind), Henry consolidated his position by vigorous efforts to reconcile the English and the Normans. He issued a charter upholding the rights of Englishmen and retracting Rufus's unpopular taxes, and he married a Scottish princess of Anglo-Saxon descent. His chief rival was his brother, Robert of Normandy, who invaded England after returning from the First Crusade in 1101. He was repulsed, and in 1106 Henry conquered Normandy, imprisoning Robert at Cardiff until his death in 1134. Henry then had to defend the duchy against Louis VI of France, who supported Robert's son.

Church and state

To end the conflict between secular and ecclesiastical authority, Henry restored Anselm as Archbishop of Canterbury. But Anselm refused to do homage to the Crown for church estates and again sought sanctuary abroad. Generally diplomatic, Henry accepted a compromise in 1107.

The *White Ship*

Henry's life was blighted in 1120 when the *White Ship*, bearing both his sons, foundered on a rock near the port of Barfleur in Normandy. This family tragedy set off a chain of events that ended in the worst of all possible circumstances for a country: the first of the three English civil wars.

Henry had lost his only legitimate son. He now made his barons swear to accept his daughter, Matilda, as his heir. Matilda, also known as Maud, would turn out to be an extremely formidable woman, but she was a woman nonetheless, and the twelfth century, with its continuous quarrels and wars, was not thought to be the time for a queen to occupy the throne. She never did become queen, but her son would eventually succeed the throne as Henry II.

Henry I died in 1135 of 'a surfeit of lampreys', no doubt food poisoning.

Henry I on hearing news of his sons' death

Stephen

must know

Born: Blois, c.1097
Parents: Stephen, Count of Blois, and Adela, daughter of William I
Ascended the throne: 22 December 1135
Coronation: Westminster Abbey, 26 December 1135
Authority: King of England
Married: Matilda, daughter of Eustace III, Count of Boulogne
Children: Three sons and two daughters
Died: Dover, 25 October 1154
Buried: Faversham Abbey

did you know?

Stephen was a man of much charm and grace and succeeded in persuading the Church authorities and the barons, who needed little encouragement, that they needed a male monarch. Stephen also had powerful friends, one of whom swore that King Henry had, on his deathbed, changed his mind about Matilda's succession to the throne. Stephen was anointed king shortly after.

Stephen was Count of Boulogne through his wife and held large estates on both sides of the Channel. When Henry died suddenly, Stephen was in Boulogne, only a day's journey from London and nearer than other possible claimants. He was accepted by the Londoners and, with most of the English barons behind him, seized the throne, disregarding his oath of fealty to Henry's daughter, Matilda. Stephen could have arrested Matilda when she landed at Arundel in 1141, but he allowed her to join her supporters in Bristol. The resulting civil war lasted 18 years. When Matilda gained the upper hand in April 1141, Stephen was briefly deposed and imprisoned. But Matilda proved even less popular and by December Stephen was back on the throne. He was crowned again, in Canterbury, and a third time at Lincoln in 1146.

Silver penny of Stephen

Difficult decisions

The great Norman barons held lands in England and Normandy. As Matilda's husband, Geoffrey of Anjou, had conquered Normandy by 1144, they were faced with a difficult decision. If loyal to Stephen, they lost their Norman estates, if to Matilda, their English ones.

Stephen

Matilda, 'the Empress'

Born: London, February 1102
Parents: Henry I and Matilda of Scotland
Ascended the throne: (22 December 1135)
Coronation: Never crowned
Married: (1) Henry V, Holy Roman Emperor, (2) Geoffrey IV, Count of Anjou
Children: With (2), three sons, including Henry II
Died: Normandy, 10 September 1167
Buried: Fontrevault Abbey

Matilda was so unpopular that her many enemies did their utmost to ensure that the crown of England would never be hers. Her arch enemy, Stephen, finally managed to capture her within the confines of Oxford Castle, but he had not reckoned on Matilda's cunning. One freezing night in December 1142 she had herself lowered down the castle walls by rope and escaped on foot across a frozen river.

The supporters of Matilda in England were led by her half-brother, Robert of Gloucester. After the Empress, as Matilda was called, arrived in England in 1141, they captured Stephen at Lincoln, and Matilda was proclaimed 'Lady of the English' rather than queen. Stubborn and haughty, she antagonized many people and soon lost London. Stephen regained the initiative and the Crown. In 1148 Matilda retired to Normandy, which her husband, Geoffrey of Anjou, had conquered, and never came back.

Stalemate

Neither side in the civil war could gain a decisive victory, but the constitutional problem was resolved, after the death of Stephen's son Eustace, by the Treaty of Westminster (1153). Stephen remained king but acknowledged Matilda's son Henry as his heir. (Stephen had another son living, but he did not want to be king.)

♕ When Matilda marched triumphant into London, the citizens – provoked by her arrogance – drove her from the city and she was forced to flee to Oxford.
♕ The Empress agreed to release Stephen after his capture at Lincoln in 1141in exchange for Robert of Gloucester (died 1147), who was held by Stephen's supporters.
♕ Matilda's husband, Geoffrey of Anjou, gave his name to the next royal dynasty, the 'Angevins'.

Geoffrey of Anjou

The Angevins (The Plantagenets)

The Angevins took their name from Geoffrey of Anjou, husband of the Empress Matilda and father of Henry II. From the fifteenth century they were also called Plantagents. According to tradition, this too derived from Geoffrey. He gained the nickname 'Plantagenet' because he used to wear a sprig of bloom, *Planta genista*, in his hat.

Farther back, legend says, the Angevins were descended from a witch, who married the Count of Anjou but disappeared when required to attend Mass. The Angevins reigned in England until the end of the fifteenth century. Although the succession was not always smooth and rebellion and civil conflict were not infrequent, the power of the Crown was greater than in any other European kingdom, including France. It represented the unity of England, which was steadily becoming a nation, and there was no doubt that the king was a very special figure. Few people would have contradicted Shakespeare's Richard II: 'There's such divinity doth hedge a king...'. The ceremony of coronation stressed this religious aspect.

The murder of Becket

The monarch's authority stretched to every part of the kingdom. Landholders and office-holders alike were dependent on royal support and approval.

Royal government was changing and becoming more complex. One result was that kings became less peripatetic, tending to settle in or around London, especially at Westminster, the site of the royal shrine (Westminster Abbey), of developing government departments and of meetings of 'parliament'.

Richard I

Henry II

> **must know**
>
> **Born:** Le Mans, 5 March 1133
> **Parents:** Geoffrey of Anjou and the Empress Matilda
> **Ascended the throne:** 25 October 1154
> **Coronation:** Westminster Abbey, 19 December 1154
> **Authority:** King of England, Duke of Normandy, Duke of Aquitaine, other titles
> **Married:** Eleanor, daughter of William X, Duke of Aquitaine, and former wife of King Louis VII of France
> **Children:** Four sons, including the future kings Richard I and John, and three daughters; other illegitimate children
> **Died:** Chinon, near Tours, 6 July 1189
> **Buried:** Fontrevault Abbey

Henry held vast dominions in France, including, through Queen Eleanor, Aquitaine, and he was the first English king for over a century to inherit the Crown without opposition. His first task was to recover royal authority and restore order and prosperity. A vagrant spirit all his life, he initially travelled widely around his empire, establishing first-hand contact with his people. He campaigned in the north, regaining land from the Scots, in Wales and in Ireland, where he was accepted as king. Triumphant in the north, though not in the west, the problems of Wales and Ireland, too, rumbled on. The English heartland, however, remained untroubled by war until 1173, when the king's increasingly ambitious sons, encouraged by Queen Eleanor and supported by the King of France, forced their father to take up arms.

He spent most of his reign on the continent, where he further extended his family's estates. His last years were marred by the rebellions of his sons.

Peace and justice

Intelligent, determined and energetic, Henry is remembered as a great reformer, a founder of English common law, and creator of sound administration and justice. All this is true, for Henry as king was a thorough professional, but, like most medieval kings, he was more interested in dynastic politics than the routines of government and law.

A flirtatious queen

Eleanor was still only 15 when she married her first husband, King Louis VII of France. King Louis was a jealous husband and it was said that her flirtatious conduct caused fierce quarrels between them. Their heirless marriage was annulled in 1152, after almost 15 years.

Eleanor was 11 years older than Henry, and is said to have seduced him, although, as she was a great heiress, that was probably not difficult. Henry was notoriously unfaithful to his wife, and they eventually separated. The Queen died in Normandy in 1204 at the age of 82. Henry was exhausted after 34 years as king, and news that his favourite son, John, had joined a rebellion is said to have hastened his death.

Henry II

Richard I

must know

Born: Beaumont Palace, Oxford, 8 September 1157
Parents: Henry II and Eleanor of Aquitaine
Ascended the throne: 6 July 1189
Coronation: Westminster Abbey, 2/3 September 1189
Authority: King of England, Duke of Normandy, Duke of Aquitaine, other titles
Married: Berengaria, daughter of Sancho V of Navarre and granddaughter of Alfonso VII of Castile
Children: Two illegitimate sons
Died: Limousin, 6 April 1199
Buried: Fontrevault Abbey

did you know?

Richard I earned his reputation and name through his extraordinary skill and leadership on the battlefield. Records compiled by churchmen heaped praise on him for his part in the Third Crusade, but neglected to mention his failure as a king. He put much of England up for sale during his reign, selling estates, lands and titles to the highest bidder in his desperate attempts to raise money to support his battles overseas.

Richard I, the Lionheart, has been highly praised by historians. However, he had an advantage: the history of his time was written by churchmen who clearly approved of the part he played in the Crusades. What they omitted to record was the fact that Richard I was one of the most neglectful kings England ever had, spending less than a year of his reign in England.

He certainly derved his military reputation, but though fighting qualities were vital in a medieval king, Richard totally failed to fill the rest of the royal bill. He had little interest in England, and none in the business of government at which his father had been so expert. Richard far preferred his Duchy of Aquitaine to England, inherited from his mother, Queen Eleanor. When he did spend time in his kingdom, for the most part, it was for the purpose of financing the Crusades.

At the start of the Third Crusade, he was allied with Philip Augustus of France, as he had been at the time of his succession following rebellion against his father. As one of the leaders of the Third Crusade, he set out for the Holy Land in 1190, won some famous victories including one against the famous Muslim commander, Saladin, but failed to recapture Jerusalem. On his way home he was captured in Austria and held prisoner for 14 months, until ransomed at great cost. During his imprisonment, Philip regained much French territory while, in England, Richard's brother John attempted to displace him. With his remarkable military abilities, Richard regained most of what had been lost before dying of a wound suffered besieging a castle near Limoges.

The end of the Angevin Empire

If Richard, the greatest warrior-king in Europe, had not died in 1199, the battle between Angevin and Capetian (the French royal house) for dominance in France might have ended differently. Richard is often blamed for neglecting England and draining it of resources, but his first duty was to his dynastic inheritance.

Sins of Sodom

♛ Richard's sexual orientation has been much debated. Churchmen tended to preach to him on the fate of the Biblical Sodom, and it was rumoured that he preferred the Queen's brother to the Queen. However, he had at least one, probably two, illegitimate children.

♛ Richard chose excellent servants, and good government was not neglected under the wise rule of Hubert Walter (died 1205), Archbishop of Canterbury.

Richard I

John

must know

Born: Beaumont Palace, Oxford, 24 December 1166
Parents: Henry II and Eleanor of Aquitaine
Ascended the throne: 6 April 1199
Coronation: Westminster Abbey, 27 May 1199
Authority: King of England and Ireland, other titles
Married: (1) Isabella of Gloucester (annulled 1199), (2) Isabella, daughter of the Count of Angoulême
Children: With (2), two sons, including the future Henry III, and three daughters; other illegitimate children
Died: Newark, 18 October 1216
Buried: Worcester Cathedral

Few English kings have been so denigrated as King John. His supposed schemings were legion and his life was punctuated with deceits. His reign was littered with humiliating battlefield defeats that saw dominion after dominion lost to France.

For example, the legends of the outlaw Robin Hood have pictured a greedy, treacherous monarch, trying by all nefarious means to undermine his illustrious brother.

John was made King of Ireland by his father in 1177. When Richard I died without an heir, the English and Norman barons chose John, while other French vassals preferred Arthur of Brittany, his nephew. John disposed of Arthur, perhaps ordering his murder, and regained part of the French possessions, but was formally dispossessed by Philip Augustus in a legal judgment of 1202. In the ensuing wars John eventually lost virtually all the hard-won territories of Angevin, including Normandy, that his brother had spent many years defending.

Papal interdict

John's refusal to accept Stephen Langton as Archbishop of Canterbury antagonized Pope Innocent III, who laid the kingdom under an interdict (no church services), 1208-13, and excommunicated the King. No one took much notice, but the withdrawal of the Church's approval inspired enemies and rebels.

Magna Carta

John provoked the English barons into revolt, though their economic difficulties through high inflation were not his fault. Civil war broke out, and John was forced to sign the document later known as Magna Carta, or 'Great Charter'. It was signed by John on the island of Runnymede in the Thames in 1216. The document was drawn up by the King's barons; it outlined their grievances and stated their rights and privileges. The Magna Carta put a temporary stop to the conflict between the barons and the monarch.

👑 Traditionally the most unpopular of kings, John has found greater approval among some recent historians.

👑 John had charm but, spoiled as a child, no tact. Aged 18, he had to be recalled from Ireland after mocking the dress and customs of Irish princes.

👑 Legend records how, taking a short cut across the Wash in 1216, John lost the crown jewels when caught out by the tide.

King John hunting

Henry III

must know

Born: Winchester, 1 October 1207
Parents: King John and Isabella of Angoulême
Ascended the throne: 18 October 1216
Coronation: Gloucester Cathedral, 28 October 1216
Authority: King of England, Ireland and parts of France
Married: Eleanor, daughter of Raymond Berenger IV, Count of Provence
Children: Six sons, including the future Edward I, and three daughters
Died: Westminster, 16 November 1272
Buried: Westminster Abbey

Henry was the first of five kings of England to succeed to the throne in childhood. The accession of a child-king brought its own problems when ambitious nobles vied to take control of his kingdom. Henry, unfortunately for his kingdom, not only came to the throne as a child but also grew up to be misguided.

The nine-year-old Henry came to the throne at an unfortunate time, with a rebellion in full swing. Moreover, he had to be crowned with his mother's torque since his father had lost the crown. Things hardly improved when he grew old enough to rule, in 1232. By the Treaty of Paris (1259) he finally surrendered his claims to Normandy and Anjou, and did homage to Louis IX of France for Gascony. At home, opposition was provoked by his choice of advisers (too many foreign relatives) and excessive expenditure. The barons took the government into their own hands, forcing the king to accept the Provisions of Oxford (1258). When he reneged, they rebelled (1264), led by Simon de Montfort, Earl of Leicester. After a brief 'reign', Simon was defeated by Henry's son, Edward, at Evesham (1265). With Henry growing senile, Edward became the effective ruler.

Henry presiding at Parliament

Parliament

The king's Great Council became known as 'parliament' during Henry's reign. Its growth resulted from the Crown's need for tax revenue. Representatives of the shires and the towns attended the parliament summoned during the Barons' War by Earl Simon in 1265.

A kingdom for a son

A prime example of Henry's misjudgement was his scheme to make his second son, Edmund, King of Sicily (1254). Requiring vast expenditure – and a campaign to oust the existing king – it appeared highly impractical and provoked the barons into taking over the government in 1258.

👑 The king's nickname, Henry the Simple, reflected his basically mild nature, artistic interests and piety.

👑 Though an inept ruler, Henry III was a cultured man and a patron of the arts, initiating the rebuilding of Edward the Confessor's Abbey of Westminster in glorious style.

👑 Tournaments were great social occasions as well as sources of popular entertainment during Henry's reign. They brought the arts of war onto the sports field and became staged, but still highly dangerous, diisplays of fighting skills.

👑 By his own wish, Henry was buried in the coffin of Edward the Confessor, its original incumbent having been removed to a grander one.

Henry III being crowned

weblink: http://www.bbc.co.uk/history/historic_figures/henry_iii_king.shtml

Edward I

must know

Born: Westminster, 17 June 1239
Parents: Henry III and Eleanor of Provence
Ascended the throne: 20 November 1272
Coronation: Westminster Abbey, 19 August 1274
Authority: King of England, Wales, Scotland and Ireland
Married: (1) Eleanor, daughter of Ferdinand III of Castile,
(2) Margaret, daughter of Philip III of France (1299)
Children: With (1), four sons, including the future Edward II,
and 12 daughters; with (2), two sons and one daughter
Died: Burgh-by-Sands, Cumbria, 7 July 1307
Buried: Westminster Abbey

did you know?

A warrior king, Edward I was responsible for creating one of the first professional English armies. The men were equipped with the revolutionary weapon of the day, the longbow, and were trained so that they could employ it effectively against the hostile forces of Wales and France. Edward's military foresight enabled him to bring Wales, Scotland and Ireland under English rule.

Sometimes called Longshanks, Edward I was a giant of a man. Yet it was not only his physique, but also his deeds in war and peace that lifted him well above the common run of English medieval kings.

Edward revived the dynasty after two ineffectual kings. King in all but name since 1265, Edward was returning from a crusade when his father died. With few French possessions except Gascony, he concentrated on asserting his sovereignty in Britain. Eight years' campaigning in Wales (1276-84) ended Welsh independence, reinforced by an unparalleled programme of castle-building to inhibit future revolts. In 1290 he asserted his overlordship of Scotland, and embarked on a series of domineering campaigns, earning the name 'Hammer of the Scots', confiscating the Stone of Scone, and provoking a long, disastrous war.

Edward I with monks and bishops

Royal justice

A forceful ruler, Edward established law and order in England, curbing the power of Church and barons and raising taxes through parliament. The so-called Model Parliament of 1295 was the most widely representative body yet summoned. The developing courts of the King's Bench, and Common Pleas furthered royal justice.

The *Hundred Rolls*

Edward ordered an administrative review of his realm in 1279, seeking to discover facts and figures concerning land usage in southern and eastern England. It was the first such large-scale enquiry since the compilation of the *Domesday Book* nearly two centuries earlier. The results were summarised in the *Hundred Rolls*, which came to be known as the 'ragman rolls' because of their raggedy appearance.

Edward and Eleanor

Edward was devoted to his wife Eleanor and when she died, near Grantham in 1290, he erected twelve memorial crosses marking the route of her cortège to London. Three of these crosses still stand. His second marriage was also happy. Edward produced more legitimate children than any other monarch.

👑 In 1273 Edward did homage to Philip III 'for all the lands which I ought to hold' in France, an ambiguous oath.

👑 At Caernarfon in 1284, according to legend, Edward proclaimed his only living new-born son, 'Prince of Wales', pointing out that he 'spoke no English'.

👑 In 1290 Edward expelled the Jews from England.

The siege of Berwick during Edward's Scottish campaign

Edward II

must know

Born: Caernarfon, 25 April 1284
Parents: Edward I and Eleanor of Castile
Ascended the throne: 8 July 1307
Coronation: Westminster Abbey, 25 February 1308
Authority: King of England, other claims
Married: Isabella, daughter of Philip IV of France
Children: Two sons, including the future Edward III, and two daughters
Died: Berkeley Castle, 21 September 1327
Buried: Gloucester Cathedral

Eccentricity was permissible in a successful monarch, but Edward's idiosyncrasies far outweighed his statecraft. His assumed lover, Piers Gaveston, a Gascon, irritated the English court, and Gaveston's murder by his enemies in 1312 was widely applauded.

It turned Edward irrevocably against the ruling class. His next favourites, the Despensers (father and son), were more acceptable, but their intrigues against the Queen induced her withdrawal to her native France. She returned in 1326 with her lover Roger Mortimer and an army. The Despensers were captured and executed, Edward was imprisoned, forced to abdicate and later murdered.

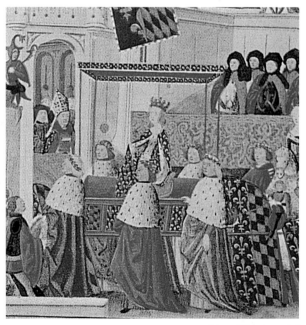

Edward II is crowned

Scottish independence

Edward belatedly continued his father's war against the Scots. Though not unathletic (reputedly a good swimmer), he was no warrior, and was not present when his army was annihilated by the Scots, led by Robert Bruce, at Bannockburn in 1314. The battle assured Scottish independence.

A grim end

Edward was murdered in a peculiarly nasty manner. A horn was inserted into his rectum, and a red-hot spit thrust through it. His corpse was unmarked. Reports of this beastly act caused a belated surge of popular sympathy for Edward and hatred for Isabella – the 'She-Wolf of France' – who spent the rest of her life confined in Castle Rising (near King's Lynn).

ꙮ Edward's difficulties after 1314 were aggravated by poor harvests and epidemics among livestock.
ꙮ Naïve and tactless, it was said that Edward enjoyed humble company and had even helped dig ditches when he should have been at Mass.
ꙮ Edward's forced abdication set an ominous precedent.

Isabella, Edward's wife

Edward III

Born: Windsor Castle, 13 November 1312

Parents: Edward II and Isabella of France

Ascended the throne: 25 January 1327

Coronation: Westminster Abbey, 29 January 1327

Authority: King of England, other claims

Married: Philippa, daughter of the Count of Hainault

Children: Eight sons, including Edward the Black Prince and John of Gaunt, and five daughters

Died: Sheen Palace, Surrey, 21 June 1377

Buried: Westminster Abbey

The origins of the Hundred Years' War lay in the Norman invasion of 1066. The French kings wanted the English territories on French soil that were being ruled under the feudal system in order to expand their empire. Many battles were fought, most famously at Crécy in 1346 and Poitiers in 1356. Longbows and cannons helped secure victory.

Edward was a warrior-king in his grandfather's mould. In spite of heavy taxation to fund war, he developed into a genial, pragmatic and popular monarch, but his determination to re-establish the greatness of his dynasty led the Crown into the long pursuit of a futile goal – the throne of France. Edward's claim through his mother was not recognized in France. England became embroiled in the so-called Hundred Years' War – actually a series of wars from 1337 to 1453. Naval victory at Sluys (1340) gave England control of the Channel. The English were victorious at Crécy (1346) and Poitiers (1356), where they were led by Edward's eldest son, the Black Prince (1330-76).

The Hundred Years' War

The Hundred Years' War was a series of English-French conflicts over possession of the French crown and land. Ultimately, the war favoured the French. By 1558 they had ended all English claims to their territory.

Edward III

♕ In 1340 Edward assumed the title, maintained by his successors until 1801, of King of France.

♕ The only permanent gain from Edward's French wars was Calais. Its capture meant a humiliating surrender for its people: six men were sent to hand over the keys of the town, barefoot with nooses around their necks, begging for mercy.

♕ In 1348-50 about one-third of the population of England died of bubonic plague in the Black Death.

Lords and Commons

Certain English institutions took recognizable form during Edward III's reign. Parliament was divided into two houses, and the procedure of impeachment was used against corrupt or incompetent ministers. Edward founded the Order of the Garter (1348), justices of the peace acquired more formal status, and English gradually replaced French as the 'official' language.

Alice Perrers

After the death of the amiable Queen Philippa (1369), Edward acquired a mistress, Alice Perrers, who shared his bed with her daughter. She is said to have infected him with gonorrhoea and, when he died after a stroke, to have stripped his body of jewels.

A Knight of the Garter

Richard II

must know

Born: 6 January 1367
Parents: Edward the Black Prince and Joan, the 'Fair Maid of Kent'
Ascended the throne: 22 June 1377
Coronation: Westminster Abbey, 16 July 1377
Authority: King of England
Married: (1) Anne of Bohemia, daughter of the Emperor Charles IV, (2) Isabella, seven-year-old daughter of Charles VI of France (1396)
Children: None
Died: Pontefract Castle, 14 February 1400
Buried: King's Langley, removed to Westminster Abbey in 1413

Richard, known as Richard of Bordeaux, succeeded his grandfather when aged ten. The chief power behind the throne was his uncle, John of Gaunt. The young king showed acumen and courage in confronting Wat Tyler, a leader of the Peasants' Revolt (1381), but lacked the capacity to control his uncles and other great lords. He antagonized many by arbitrary and unpredictable decisions and hefty poll taxes. While the king was in Ireland in 1399 John of Gaunt's son, Henry Bolingbroke, whom he had banished, invaded northern England and rallied enough support to force Richard's abdication in his favour (1399). Richard died a prisoner the following year, either through self-starvation or as a victim of murder.

That the king should be succeeded by his eldest son had become well established. Primogeniture reduced conflict over the succession, but sometimes placed a child on the throne. The unfortunate Richard was overshadowed by the formidable sons of Edward III, all too ambitious to be a father substitute.

Culture and cookery

Richard, who is said to have invented the handkerchief, was passionately interested in dress, fine cooking and books. He presided over an exotically luxurious court, very different from his predecessors', at the centre of a remarkable flowering of English literature and art. The finest works of Geoffrey Chaucer, William Langland and John Gower were written during Richard's reign

The father of English poetry

Geoffrey Chaucer was the greatest English writer of medieval times, arguably unmatched until William Shakespeare (1564-1616). Chaucer's *Canterbury Tales*, with its keen observation of character, its humour and its ingenious plots, still retains its popularity more than 600 years after it was written. Chaucer, however, was much more than a brilliant writer. He was also a linguist, courtier, diplomat, adviser to kings, and a close friend of John of Gaunt. His fluency in Italian, French and Latin, as well as his knowledge of law and royal courts stood him in good stead for a position such as this. He was aide to kings Edward III, Richard II and Henry IV.

✦ Criticism of the king's advisers, meaning the royal government in general, reached a peak in the 'Merciless Parliament' (1388).

✦ Richard's court cookery book, called *The Forme of Cury*, contained recipes for dishes such as oysters in Greek wine.

✦ When Queen Anne died in Sheen Palace in 1394, Richard's grief and rage were such that he had the building levelled.

Richard taken to the Tower

Henry IV

must know

Born: Bolingbroke Castle, 4 April 1366
Parents: John of Gaunt and Blanche of Lancaster
Ascended the throne: 30 Sept 1399
Coronation: Westminster Abbey, 13 Oct 1399
Authority: King of England
Married: (1) Mary de Bohun, daughter of the Earl of Hereford, (2) Joan, daughter of Charles II of Navarre
Children: With (1), five sons, including the future Henry V, and two daughters
Died: Westminster Abbey, 20 March 1413
Buried: Canterbury Cathedral

Henry Bolingbroke succeeded his father, who died in 1399, as Duke of Lancaster and overthrew Richard II, who had seized the Lancastrian estates. As king, he was – predictably as a usurper – confronted by revolt and conspiracy himself. More energetic and more conciliatory than Richard, he overcame all opponents, defeating supporters of Richard II (1399), the powerful Percys of Northumberland (1408), and, most formidably, Owain Glyndw in Wales. The French took the opportunity to raid the south, and the Scots the north, but King James I of Scots was captured in 1406 and a truce with France agreed in 1407. Thereafter, Henry was relatively safe.

To the insecurity of the Crown was added the constant problem of insufficient income. Henry endured considerable criticism from parliament before it would grant the taxes he needed. His moderation and willingness to compromise ensured that, though he might not get all he wanted, he did not provoke dangerous opposition.

The young Henry Bolingbroke

Royal leper?

Short and plain, presenting a marked contrast with the elegant Richard II, Henry suffered poor health in later years and was worn out at 47. He suffered from a disfiguring skin complaint which contemporaries thought was leprosy. Medical historians now believe it was a severe form of eczema.

♕ Henry IV was the first king of the House of Lancaster. There was no dynastic break, he and his predecessor both being grandsons of Edward III.

♕ It had been prophesied that Henry would die in Jerusalem. He presumed that meant on crusade. He actually died in the abbot's parlour at Westminster Abbey, a room known as the Jerusalem Chamber.

♕ Henry IV's greatest achievement was to leave his son a kingdom that was peaceful, loyal and united.

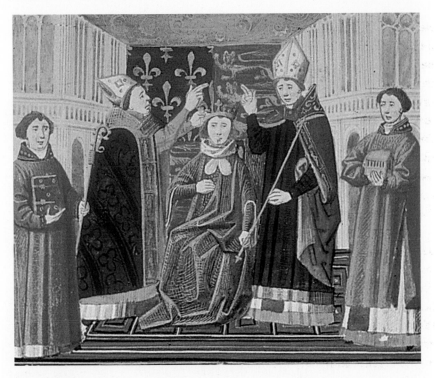

Coronation of Henry IV

Henry V

must know

Born: Monmouth, 9 August 1387
Parents: Henry IV and Mary de Bohun
Ascended the throne: 20 March 1413
Coronation: Westminster Abbey, 9 April 1413
Authority: King of England, Duke of Normandy (from 1417), Regent of France (1420)
Married: Catherine de Valois, daughter of Charles VI of France (1420)
Children: One son, the future Henry VI
Died: Vincennes, 31 August 1422
Buried: Westminster Abbey

Henry was the last, perhaps the ablest, of the medieval warrior-kings. He made England once more a continental power. He attacked France to reclaim his Angevin territories using a formidable array of weapons. His soldiers were armed with arrows, bowstaves, rudimentary canon, and swords as well as being supported by mounted cavalry. He won a sensational victory at Agincourt (1415). In 1417-19 he reconquered Normandy, advanced to Paris, and signed the Treaty of Troyes (1420), gaining Charles VI's daughter and recognition as regent and heir to the French throne. This was not popular in France, but Henry died, perhaps fortunately, before his grandiose plans of conquest could be fulfilled.

Henry and Catherine's marriage

Military genius?

The portrayal of Henry V as a great patriotic warrior was not entirely a creation by William Shakespeare in his play about the king's reign. Henry's fighting and leadership skills were considerable, as he proved in Wales during the reign of his father.

Fearless and determined, Henry was also an able strategist, and the success of his French campaign was based on two years of careful planning. He took care to ensure control of the Channel and to strengthen his position by useful alliances, especially with Burgundy.

A popular autocrat

Henry's single-minded pursuit of conquest now seems unattractive, and he was undoubtedly ruthless and authoritarian. Yet he was a hero. War was a popular activity, if you won. Henry encountered minimal opposition from England's turbulent nobility and raised extra revenue through parliament without serious difficulty.

👑 Henry's victory against heavy odds at Agincourt has been ascribed to the superiority of the longbow, allegedly a Welsh invention.

👑 Henry, personally devout, followed his father in persecuting the Lollards, Protestant dissidents.

👑 Henry died of dysentery, which probably caused more casualties in medieval armies than human foes.

Morning of Agincourt

Henry VI

<table>
<tr><td>

must know

Born: Windsor Castle, 6 December 1421
Parents: Henry V and Catherine de Valois
Ascended the throne: 1 September 1422
Coronation: Westminster Abbey, 6 November 1429;
repeated St Paul's Cathedral, 13 October 1470
Authority: King of England
Married: Margaret, daughter of the Count of Anjou
Children: One son, Edward (died 1471)
Died: Tower of London, 21 May 1471
Buried: Chertsey Abbey; removed to St George's Chapel,
Windsor, 1484

</td><td>

did you know?

Henry VI became king while he was still an infant. He is generally agreed to have been a weak and ineffective king. He was a dreamer and would have been far better suited to a monastic life – he had a gentle and scholarly personality, which made him easy prey for the main rivals for the throne, the House of York. He was captured twice during battles against the Yorkists.

</td></tr>
</table>

Henry V had been an outstanding and inspiring battlefield commander champing at the bit to be a warrior-king. His son, by contrast, was a religious, almost ascetic character, who had kingship thrust upon him when less than nine months old.

Although he was crowned King of France in Paris (1431), the conquests of Henry V were soon lost. By 1453 only Calais remained. Henry was incapable of leading an army and, partly perhaps as a result of the French disasters, suffered his first attack of insanity in 1452. Richard, Duke of York reigned as Protector until Henry recovered in 1455, when the rivalry between Lancaster and York was developing into civil war. Henry was captured in 1460, deposed in 1461, briefly restored by Richard Neville, the Earl of Warwick, 'the Kingmaker', in 1470, before being finally returned to the Tower where he was stabbed to death by an unknown hand.

Henry's second coronation

The Maid of Orléans

The French recovery was inspired by Joan of Arc and the coronation of Charles VII at Reims (1429). The English began to suffer defeats, their allies deserted them, and parliament had to provide ever-growing sums for what had become an unsuccessful war. Peace proved elusive. Even Henry's marriage to a formidable French princess in 1445 brought only a breathing space.

'A prey unto the House of York'

Henry VI was pious and well-meaning. He might have made an excellent bishop, but kingship was beyond him. He lacked his father's qualities of leadership, and allowed power to fall into the hands of an inadequate clique. His attacks of insanity may have been inherited from his maternal grandfather.

W A rising in Kent led by Jack Cade (1450), partly provoked by dislike of the King's favourites, succeeded in taking London while Henry cowered in Kenilworth Castle.

W Henry's cast of mind was prudish. When shown his baby son, he expressed surprise, remarking that he must have been conceived by the Holy Ghost.

W Henry's interest in matters of the spirit and the mind led the young king to found Eton college – its doors opening in the autumn of 1440 – and King's College, Cambridge, the foundation stone laid on 2 April 1441.

Henry VI suffered from bouts of mental instability

The Wars of the Roses

The dynastic conflict that began in the 1450s was later called the Wars of the Roses (the red rose of Lancaster versus the white rose of York). Beginning as a revolt against weak government, it became a challenge to the throne when Richard, Duke of York (1311-60) formed an alliance with the powerful Earl of Warwick.

The Yorkists won the Battle of Towton (1461) and Richard's son, Edward IV, became king. Warwick, dissatisfied with his rewards, sided with the Lancastrians in 1469, and Henry VI was briefly restored (1470-1). The efforts of Richard, Duke of Gloucester, Edward IV's younger brother and guardian of the younger Edward V, to seize the crown himself alienated Lancastrians as well as Yorkists, and his overthrow by Henry Tudor (1485) marked the end of the Wars of the Roses.

The leader of the Lancastrian cause, given the feebleness of Henry VI, was his tigerish queen, Margaret of Anjou (1429-82). After Towton she fled to France, returned with a French army, was defeated but returned again with more French soldiers, forcing Edward IV, in turn, to flee. Imprisoned in 1471, she was ransomed in 1475 and left England for good.

The war was a long and somewhat confused campaign, with the rival camps of York and Lancaster fighting over succession to the Crown for over 30 years by the time the Lancastrians won the day at Bosworth. Initially, the reasons for the civil wars had been real and justified: the corruption in the Lancastrian government was countered by the promise of just rule by the Yorkists. By the last of the battles, it had simply become a dynastic struggle between Richard III and Henry, the Earl of Richmond, a relatively unknown quantity who had spent much of his life in exile.

Edward IV in council

Edward IV

must know

Born: Rouen, 28 April 1442
Parents: Richard, Duke of York, and Cecily,
daughter of Ralph Neville, Earl of Westmorland
Ascended the throne: 4 March 1461
Coronation: Westminster Abbey, 28 June 1461
Authority: King of England
Married: Elizabeth, daughter of Richard Woodville,
Lord Rivers
Children: Three sons, including the future Edward V,
and seven daughters; four illegitimate children
Died: Westminster, 9 April 1483
Buried: St George's Chapel, Windsor

did you know?

Elizabeth Woodville married
Edward IV in 1464. She made
herself very unpopular with the
royal family by elevating the
status of her own family,
including that of her sons by her
first marriage. Edward's brother
Richard, Duke of Gloucester, was
so enraged by this that on the
king's death he destroyed her
family, beheading some for
allegedly plotting his death.
Elizabeth lived the rest of her life
in a convent.

As soon as he was old enough, Edward fought in the Yorkist cause. After his father's
death at Wakefield (1460) and the victory of Towton (1461), Henry VI was deposed and
Edward declared king. Following the alliance of Margaret of Anjou and the Earl of
Warwick, Edward was himself deposed (October 1470) and fled abroad but, with a
small army of mercenaries, he regained the throne in April 1471. It took the death of
Warwick at the Battle of Barnet, victory at Tewkesbury and the death of Henry VI and
his only son to secure Edward's throne.

His high-profile court was one of splendour and luxury, characterised by flamboyance
and hedonism. Edward's subjects were won over through flattery and the personal touch.
He went to great lengths to convert the formerly ascetic court of his predecessor into a
festive place. Popular and pleasure-loving, he was nevertheless a formidable monarch,
whose potential was extinguished by early death.

Dreams of glory

Well served by able ministers and in tune with England's increasingly prosperous
merchants, Edward conciliated parliament by abjuring special taxes and built up
commercially useful foreign connections. When his attempt to revive the claim
to France failed, he accepted a handsome payment for withdrawing his forces.

'Too good to be his harlot'

♛ Edward, rare for a monarch, married for love and got away with it.
The beautiful widow, Elizabeth Woodville (c.1437–92), who came from a family
of Lancastrian gentry, refused to be his mistress so he married her secretly
(1464), revealing the fait accompli only when he came under pressure to make
a diplomatic match.

♛ Edward's brother George, Duke of Clarence, who joined Warwick and the rebels
in 1469, was executed (or according to legend drowned in a butt of wine) in 1478.

♛ Edward's marriage and the lavish advancement of his wife's relations caused
trouble and encouraged Warwick, 'the Kingmaker', to change sides.

Edward landing in Calais

Edward V

must know

Born: Westminster, 4 November 1470
Parents: Edward IV and Elizabeth Woodville
Ascended the throne: 9 April 1483
Coronation: Not crowned
Authority: King of England
Married: Unmarried
Died: Probably the Tower of London, c.September 1483
Buried: Tower of London; possible remains reburied in Westminster Abbey, 1678

During his father's reign the young Prince of Wales was placed in the care of his mother's relations in Ludlow. Succeeding his father at the age of twelve, he was brought to London by his ruthless and ambitious uncle, Richard, Duke of Gloucester, his official guardian and Protector of the Realm. Leading members of the Woodvilles were arrested, and Edward, with his younger brother Richard, was lodged in the Tower. Prompted by Gloucester, parliament declared that Edward IV's marriage to Elizabeth Woodville had been invalid, and its issue therefore illegitimate. The young king was deposed on 25 June 1483. He and his brother were seen in the Tower in September, but never again.

The dangers of faction

The dynastic conflicts of the 15th century were largely the result of royal dependence on factions, which inevitably made enemies of those outside the magic circle. The Yorkist princes, including Edward IV, tended to behave like great lords rather than national leaders.

Richard was greatly trusted by his brother who named him Protector of his children. However Edward IV's royal relatives, including Richard, believed the king had married beneath him and, in doing so, had elevated the Woodvilles far too high above their humble rank. English history is full of ambitious relatives brought close to the throne in this fashion and who used their unaccustomed power and position for their own unscrupulous ends. The Woodvile family certainly figured among them.

The princes in the tower

The fate of the the young princes poses the most famous conundrum in English history. There seems little doubt that they were murdered and – although interesting cases have been made against others – that their uncle Richard III was responsible.

♛ There was nothing particularly sinister in the choice of the Tower as the princes' lodging. It was then a royal residence as well as a prison.

♛ In 1678 bones believed to be those of the murdered princes were discovered in the Tower. They were reinterred in Westminster Abbey on the order of Charles II.

Richard III

must know

Born: Fotheringay Castle, 2 October 1452
Parents: Richard, Duke of York, and Cecily Neville
Ascended the throne: 26 June 1483
Coronation: Westminster Abbey, 6 July 1483
Authority: King of England
Married: Anne Neville, daughter of the Earl of Warwick, the 'Kingmaker'
Children: One son, Edward (died 1484); several illegitimate children
Died: Bosworth, Leicestershire, 22 August 1485
Buried: Greyfriars Abbey, Leicester; later disinterred and desecrated, 1678

A loyal and – as Duke of Gloucester and married to a Neville – powerful supporter of his brother, Edward IV, Richard served effectively in the Borders, recapturing Berwick from the Scots. On Edward's death, he ruthlessly suppressed the Woodvilles, forcing the widowed Elizabeth to take sanctuary at Westminster, and secured the Crown for himself. He antagonized many Yorkists, including the Earl of Buckingham (executed, with other opponents, without trial in 1483). Confronted by the Lancastrian invasion force of Henry Tudor at Bosworth, and deserted at the last minute by Lord Stanley with 7000 men, he was defeated and killed.

The last Yorkist

In his brief reign Richard showed himself an able administrator, prepared to be conciliatory, more active than his predecessor but, like him, a patron of the arts.

The wicked uncle

Richard's reputation suffered through Tudor propaganda, much of it demonstrably false, and augmented by Shakespeare. He was a product of the degeneration in political behaviour since c.1450 and arguably no more ruthless than other Renaissance monarchs. Since the eighteenth century, he has had many defenders, and today his memory is rehabilitated by the Richard III Society.

👑 In spite of his nickname, 'Crouchback', Richard's disability seems to have been no more than a minor irregularity of the shoulder.

👑 Staring defeat inthe face at Bosworth, Richard refused to flee, declaring, 'I will die King of England.'

👑 During the Reformation, Richard's bones were dug up and thrown into the River Soar.

Richard III's reputation suffered at the hands of the Tudors

3 Tudors and Stuarts

The House of Tudor reigned during one of the most successful periods of England's history, and the kings and queens from this time are examined here. The Stuart line, although long established in Scotland, was by comparison less successful in England. Its ups and downs are also charted in this section.

The Tudors

The claim to the throne made by Henry VII, the first monarch of the Tudor dynasty, was tenuous: Henry's mother was descended from John of Gaunt, a son of Edward III and ancestor of the House of Lancaster. Henry also claimed descent from Welsh princes.

Compared with earlier aspirants, he was fortunate in the absence of other claimants. Richard III was dead and had no surviving children. Many Yorkist supporters, including Edward IV's widowed queen, Elizabeth Woodville, supported him, and the ruling class, after three decades of conflict, were war-weary. Henry portrayed himself as a figure of reconciliation, marrying a Yorkist princess, but, like other conquerors, he won and held the throne by his own efforts.

The House of Tudor, neatly encapsulating the 16th century by ruling from 1485 to 1603, was perhaps the most successful in English history. Its three most significant members, Henry VII, Henry VIII and Elizabeth I, who together reigned for almost 106 of those years, were all, whatever their personal qualities, highly capable rulers, though their reputation is less high among recent historians. They also reigned in a fortunate period for European monarchy (exemplified on the Continent by the Valois/Bourbon and Habsburg dynasties), when the power of the Crown was less threatened by 'overmighty subjects' and not yet seriously threatened by parliament. Among other achievements, the Tudors re-established the hereditary principle, which had seemed in danger of collapse during the 15th century.

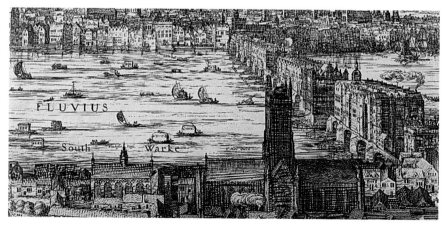

Elizabethan London

Henry VII

must know

Born: Pembroke, 28 January 1457
Parents: Edmund Tudor, Earl of Richmond, and Lady Margaret Beaufort
Ascended the throne: 22 August 1485
Coronation: Westminster Abbey, 30 October 1485
Authority: King of England
Married: Elizabeth of York, daughter of Edward IV
Children: Four sons, including the future Henry VIII, and four daughters
Died: Richmond, Surrey, 21 April 1509
Buried: Westminster Abbey

The Yorkist and Lancastrian branches of the Plantagenet royal family so decimated themselves in the Wars of the Roses that an obscure descendant of Edward III, Henry Tudor, was able to claim the throne and become Henry VII, establishing a new dynasty.

At first Henry's chances of seizing the throne seemed slight. No one seemed certain that he had any legal right to the English Crown at all. He was hidden away, spending most of his youth in Wales and in exile in Brittany.

After his victory at Bosworth he rapidly consolidated his position. Three 'pretenders', Lord Lovel, Lambert Simnel and Perkin Warbeck, appeared against him but none commanded sufficient support, and Henry restored the reputation of the monarch as one who rules, not merely reigns. His basic methods were to enforce the law, especially against magnates who exceeded their rights, and to exploit the Crown's powers of patronage. He selected his closest advisers for their loyalty and ability, especially in raising Crown revenue. As he also avoided foreign wars, Henry never needed to appeal to parliament for funds and left a full treasury.

Growing kingdom

The population was expanding, especially in London, indicating growing prosperity. Like his predecessors, Henry VII encouraged both trade, making advantageous commercial treaties, and the cloth industry. Among the enterprises he sponsored was the voyage from Bristol of John Cabot in 1497 which led to the discovery of the North America mainland.

Respected though not loved

Henry is remembered for the magnificent Perpendicular interiors of his chapel in Westminster Abbey and King's College, Cambridge. But, if not the miser critics called him, he was tough and ruthless in pursuit of his interests, and some of his expedients for raising money from his subjects were of doubtful legality. As a result, he was not popular with his subjects, some of whom greeted his death with celebration.

♛ With confident irony, Henry put the disgraced pretender Lambert Simnel to work in the royal kitchens.

♛ Henry's mother, Lady Margaret Beaufort, was a notable patron of religious and educational foundations. Her name is still gratefully remembered by the universities of Oxford and Cambridge.

♛ Great things were expected from Henry's eldest son, Arthur, Prince of Wales, but he died in 1502.

Henry VII, founder of the new Tudor dynasty

Henry VIII

must know

Born: Greenwich, 28 June 1491
Parents: Henry VII and Elizabeth of York
Ascended the throne: 21 April 1509
Coronation: Westminster Abbey, 24 June 1509
Authority: King of England and Ireland
Married: Six wives (see page 142-43)
Children: Two daughters and one son (see page 142-43); three or four illegitimate children
Died: Whitehall, 28 January 1547
Buried: St George's Chapel, Windsor

did you know?

King Henry VIII was an omnipotent monarch who delighted in public acknowledgement of his power. He believed himself to be an archtypal Renaissance king, who was an awe-inspiring leader, scholar and figurehead. He had a great love of the arts.

Handsome, intelligent, athletic, Henry appeared the perfect Renaissance prince. He added to his popularity by executing his father's hated tax collectors, Richard Empson and Edmund Dudley, but until 1529 he left mundane administration largely in the hands of Thomas Wolsey, the ambitious and able son of a Suffolk grazier. Abandoning his father's peaceful foreign policy, Henry wasted resources on flamboyant but unsuccessful expeditions against France and wars with Scotland and Spain. He recouped vast amounts by dissolving the monasteries and confiscating their property (1536-9), but squandered most of that on military expenditure in the 1540s.

Henry VIII, by Hans Holbein

Reformation

As a result of difficulties in obtaining permission to divorce from the Pope, Henry exploited widespread anticlericalism to end the authority of the Pope and place himself at the head of the English Church. This was accomplished in 1532-6 through a series of momentous Acts of Parliament, with the guidance of Thomas Cromwell, Wolsey's sucessor. One result of this revolution was to raise the constitutional status of parliament.

From prince to ogre

Henry was a second son, distrusted by his father. An inferiority complex may have been responsible for his intense egoism and extreme touchiness, which, combined with declining health and increasing megalomania, turned him from the 'Bluff King Hal' of his early years into the frightening despot of the 1540s.

♛ Ironically, Henry earned the title *Fidei Defensor*, 'Defender of the Faith', from the Pope for his pamphlet attacking Luther. The title is still held and appears, abbreviated, on modern British coins.

♛ Greed made Henry grossly fat. At Boulogne in 1544 he was carried about in a chair and hauled upstairs by machinery.

The Mary Rose

The *Mary Rose*, Henry's flagship built at Portsmouth Dockyard in 1509-10, was described by Lord High Admiral Sir Edward Howard as 'the noblest shipp of sayle and grett shipp at this hour that I trow to be in Christendom'. In defence of Portsmouth against an invading French fleet in 1545, the *Mary Rose* sank. Efforts to salvage the pride of the English fleet began at once, but sixteenth-century diving techniques were insufficient to accomplish such a huge task. It was not until 1982 that she was lifted off the seabed and returned to the surface and her remains put on display at Portsmouth.

The wives of Henry VIII

Henry VIII is the best known of English monarchs, largely because he had six wives. This unrivalled record was partly due to his character, but also to political demands and chance circumstance, such as the need to produce healthy boys. For all Henry's efforts, only three legitimate children survived him, only one of them a boy, and a sickly youth at that.

(1) **Catherine of Aragon** (1485-1536), daughter of Ferdinand II of Aragon and Isabella of Castile; widow of Prince Arthur, Henry's elder brother. She married Henry on 11 June 1509. Although the queen conceived eight times, no child survived infancy except **Mary**. By c.1525 it was obvious that Catherine would not produce a male heir. The Pope's refusal to grant an annulment set in motion the events leading to the break with Rome.

(2) **Anne Boleyn** (c.1507-36), daughter of Sir Thomas Boleyn and Lady Elizabeth Howard. She was pregnant when Henry married her on 25 January 1533. Besides **Elizabeth**, she had two still-born children and one miscarriage. Failure to produce a boy and accusations of adultery, probably just foolish flirtation, led to her execution for treason on 19 May 1536.

(3) **Jane Seymour** (c.1505-37), daughter of Sir John Seymour and Margaret Wentworth. She married Henry on 30 May 1536 and died soon after giving birth to a son, **Edward**.

(4) **Anne of Cleves** (1515-57), daughter of the Duke of Cleves. She married Henry on 6 January 1540. It was an arranged, diplomatic match and Anne proved to be much plainer than Holbein's pre-nuptial portrait of her had suggested. The marriage was annulled on 9 July 1540.

(5) **Catherine Howard** (c.1520-42), daughter of Lord Edmund Howard. She married Henry on 28 July 1540. As a high-spirited girl tied to a bloated and repellent husband, she may have been guilty, as accused, of infidelity, for which she was executed on 13 February 1542.

(6) **Catherine Parr** (c.1512-48), daughter of Sir Thomas Parr. A sensible lady already twice widowed, she married Henry on 12 July 1543. Her function was that of nurse and stepmother, roles she fulfilled admirably.

The fate of Henry's wives is commemorated in a mnemonic:
Divorced, beheaded, died,
Divorced, beheaded, survived.

Edward VI

Born: Hampton Court, 12 Oct 1537
Parents: Henry VIII and Jane Seymour
Ascended the throne: 28 January 1547
Coronation: Westminster Abbey, 19 Feb 1547
Authority: King of England and Ireland
Married: Unmarried
Died: Greenwich, 6 July 1553
Buried: Westminster Abbey

Henry VIII tried to ensure that no challenges from abroad or at home could prevent Edward from inheriting the throne. However, Edward succumbed to tuberculosis just six years after becoming king.

As Edward was only nine when his father died, his uncle, Edward Seymour, later Duke of Somerset, became Lord Protector until, having failed disastrously to carry through Henry VIII's aggressive schemes in Scotland, he was displaced in 1550 (executed 1552) by John Dudley, Earl of Warwick, who appointed himself Duke of Northumberland.

Always frail, Edward, whose name is commemorated in numerous grammar schools founded during his reign, died at 15, probably of tuberculosis.

Edward VI

Reformation continued

During Edward's reign, the Henrician Reformation was carried through to its logical conclusion when the English Church adopted Protestantism with the introduction of the First Book of Common Prayer (1549), compiled by Thomas Cramner, Archbishop of Canterbury.

Precocious youth

Edward was intensively educated by leading scholars, who inclined him towards the reformed religion and turned him into a learned young pedant. He enjoyed a short family life with his sisters under the amiable tutelage of Catherine Parr.

The 'Nine Days' Queen

In pursuit of his family ambitions, the Duke of Northumberland persuaded Edward to will the Crown to **Lady Jane Grey** (1537-54). A Protestant, she was the granddaughter of Henry VIII's sister, Mary, and was married to Northumberland's son, Lord Guildford Dudley. She was proclaimed queen on Edward's death. Northumberland's scheme fell flat when neither Lords nor Commons would accept her and declared for the rightful heir, Mary. Jane and her husband were executed on 12 February 1554. Northumberland, who unlike Jane had recanted in an effort to save his head, preceded them to the block in 1553.

Lady Jane Grey's execution

Mary I

<table>
<tr>
<td>

must know

Born: Greenwich Palace, 8 February 1516
Parents: Henry VIII and Catherine of Aragon
Ascended the throne: 19 July 1553
Coronation: Westminster Abbey, 1 October 1553
Authority: Queen of England and Ireland
Married: Philip II of Spain
Children: None
Died: Whitehall, 17 November 1558
Buried: Westminster Abbey

</td>
<td>

did you know?

The marriage of Queen Mary and Philip of Spain was strongly objected to by the majority of her subjects, but it went ahead in 1554 despite the opposition. She hoped that her union with a Catholic would return Protestant England to Catholicism. The wedding stool used during the ceremony is now in Winchester Cathedral.

</td>
</tr>
</table>

Half-Spanish and a devout Roman Catholic, Mary married the future King of Spain, Philip II, as his second wife, in 1554. The marriage was unpopular and provoked Wyatt's Rebellion. Mary's great aim was to restore the authority of the Pope and return the country to Roman Catholicism. She earned her nickname 'Bloody Mary' for her unrelenting persecution of Protestants. Some of these, such as Archbishop Thomas Cranmer, were political victims; others were militants of a kind who would have been burned under Henry VIII. Mary's failure to produce an heir assured a Protestant future.

Bloody Mary

Mary was strong willed, a shrewd politician and believed passionately that it was her duty to return England to the Catholic Church. In Mary's five-year reign around 300 Protestants were put to death by burning for refusing to convert to Catholicism. Because of this, Mary acquired the nickname 'Bloody Mary'.

Calais Lost

In 1557 Philip, now King of Spain, made a short visit to England, enlisting the country in his war against France. The result was the loss of Calais (1558), the last remaining English possession in France. Mary said that when she died the words 'Philip' and 'Calais' would be found engraved upon her heart.

An unhappy union

Mary, who had once been courted by her husband's father, Charles V, was devoted to Philip though he found her repellent. She insisted that he should have the title of king and, although he spent more time in Spain, both their names appeared on Acts of Parliament and both their faces on the coinage. So desperate was she for a child that in 1555 she convinced herself she was pregnant.

♕ Mary had a difficult childhood. Having been the king's adored little girl, she became a thorn in his side. After Henry's divorce from her mother, Mary was threatened, mistreated, starved and abused by the king and his court.

♕ Execution by burning, a particularly cruel method, was reintroduced in February 1555.

Mary I died hated and reviled

Elizabeth I

must know

Born: Greenwich, 7 September 1533
Parents: Henry VIII and Anne Boleyn
Ascended the throne: 17 November 1558
Coronation: Westminster Abbey, 15 January 1559
Authority: Queen of England and Ireland
Married: Unmarried
Children: None
Died: Richmond Palace, Surrey, 24 March 1603
Buried: Westminster Abbey

did you know?

The coronation of Elizabeth I marked the beginning of a great reign. Elizabeth dedicated her life to her people, so much so that she declared that she was married to her kingdom and would therefore not take a husband. She did, however, flirt with foreign suitors, when she could these important contacts to her advantage.

Elizabeth, England's most popular ruler, had a difficult childhood, having been declared illegitimate after the fall of Anne Boleyn. Under Mary she was a prisoner, held briefly in the Tower, as a likely focus of Protestant plots. She proved to be a ruler of quality: courageous, shrewd and possessing a potent way with words, although she was politically indecisive. Historically she benefited from the extraordinary cult of 'Gloriana' created around her by courtiers, and from the exceptional quality of Elizabethan mariners, poets (including Shakespeare) and other Renaissance heroes who ornamented her long and prosperous reign. Her aim was stability and concord, but administration was neglected. Crown revenue declined, corruption crept in to government, and a rift began to open between Crown and parliament.

Execution of Mary, Queen of Scots

The deposed Mary, Queen of Scots, would not have survived in captivity in England as long as she did without the mercy of her cousin, Elizabeth. Loath to execute a fellow monarch, Elizabeth repeatedly refused to sign Mary's death warrant. Catholic hopes relied on Mary retrieving the English throne from the Protestant Elizabeth. Consequently Mary became embroiled in plots. Several of these schemes were hatched and encouraged by King Phillip II of Spain, Elizabeth's former brother-in-law. When, in 1586, another plot was hatched by a young Catholic called Anthony Babington, it came at a time when England stood in grave danger of invasion from Spain. It was this that finally sealed Mary's fate.

The Thirty-Nine Articles

Elizabeth's major achievement was the settlement of the religious question, with the creation of the Church of England, based on the Thirty-Nine Articles (1563). However, it automatically turned English Catholics into traitors, and displeased those radical Protestants who came to be known as Puritans.

The Virgin Queen

Although Elizabeth had many suitors, and was romantically involved with Sir Robert Dudley, Earl of Leicester, she never married. She was able to exploit her availability to some advantage, and it augmented her popularity, always carefully courted, with the common people. Yet spinsterhood may have been due to personal preference as well as statecraft.

♛ Philip II of Spain, England's former king, now enemy, launched an invasion fleet, the famous Spanish Armada in 1588, but it was broken up by the navy and storms.

♛ Elizabeth's portraits show not so much a woman or even a queen as a gorgeous icon.

♛ Elizabeth kept the note Leicester had written to her from Rycote a few days before his death in a little casket by her bed, where it was found after her own death, fifteen years later. Across it she had written 'his last letter'.

Elizabeth I, the
'Virgin Queen'

The Stuarts

The Stewart, or Stuart, dynasty, long established in Scotland, was not very successful in England, especially by comparison with the Tudors. In spite of inheriting a Crown that seemed more secure than any in Europe, two of the four Stuart kings lost it, and one of them, Charles I, lost his head as well. For a time (the first – and last – time since the Anglo-Saxons), Britain had no monarchy at all.

The Stuart monarchs all had defects of character. In some cases those defects were not only glaringly apparent but politically dangerous. All the same, the unfortunate record of the dynasty cannot be ascribed to such simple causes alone. Although the Stuart period appears dominated by the civil conflicts of the middle decades of the 17th century, great though less obvious changes were taking place in society – changes, some historians argue, of greater significance than the sensational events of the civil wars. The monarchy as inherited by the Stuarts commanded enormous powers, but it was ill-equipped to understand or regulate these changes, and the resources at its disposal were insufficient to carry out the tasks it was expected to perform. Thanks to taxes on trade, revenue was just sufficient to govern the country in peacetime, but not enough in time of war. Additional revenue could only be raised through parliament, but parliament was increasingly critical of royal government, and inclined to attach unacceptable conditions to its grants. Gradually, disagreement spiralled into open war.

James I

James I

must know

Ascended the throne: 24 March 1603
Coronation: Westminster Abbey, 25 July 1603
Authority: King of Great Britain and Ireland
Married: Anne, daughter of Frederick II of Denmark and Norway (1589)
Children: Three sons, including the future Charles I, and five daughters
Died: Theobalds Park, Hertfordshire, 27 March 1625
Buried: Westminster Abbey

For James's early life and reign in Scotland, see James VI, King of Scots, page 41. Scholarly but unkingly, James irritated some courtiers by his informal habits and homosexual inclinations. He soon came into conflict with Puritans in the Church and narrow-minded squires in parliament, and his vision of himself as a symbol of unity between his three kingdoms and between the Scottish and English Churches was unrealized. The outbreak of the Thirty Years War (1618) and war with Spain (1624) spoiled his efforts as a peacemaker, and the planting of Protestant Scots and English in Ulster stored up future troubles. But the kingdom was peaceful and secure, religious and other conflicts diminished, and the fundamental authority of the Crown was unchallenged.

To Virginia

In James's reign the first permanent English colonies were established in Virginia (named for the 'Virgin Queen'). Jamestown was sponsored by London merchants and founded in 1607. The first colony in New England was established by the Pilgrim Fathers, a group of idealistic religious dissidents who sailed on the *Mayflower* in 1620.

Royal favourites

After the death of the capable royal servant, Robert Cecil, Lord Salisbury, in 1612, James tended to rely on favourites. They included the dubious Robert Carr, Earl of Somerset, who became involved in a murder case, and the handsome but pretentious George Villiers, Duke of Buckingham, assassinated in 1628.

♛ An auspicious result of the Hampton Court conference on religious affairs (1604) was the commissioning of an authorized version of the Bible – the King James Bible.

♛ James's queen, Anne of Denmark, led a largely separate life, enjoying royal 'progresses' around the country.

♛ James's support for the episcopalian system of Church government was enshrined in his phrase, 'No bishop, no king'.

Charles I

must know

Born: Dunfermline, 19 November 1600
Parents: James VI and I and Anne of Denmark
Ascended the throne: 27 March 1625
Coronation: Westminster Abbey, 2 February 1626
Authority: King of Great Britain and Ireland
Married: Henrietta Maria, daughter of Henri IV of France
Children: Four sons, including the future Charles II and James II, and five daughters
Died: Whitehall, 30 January 1649
Buried: St George's Chapel, Windsor

Charles was a frail and backward child who became heir apparent on the death of his promising elder brother, Henry, in 1612. Encountering opposition in parliament, he ruled without it during the 'Eleven Years Tyranny' (1629-40), levying taxes unsanctioned by parliament. A revolt by the Scots, provoked by measures to align the Presbyterian Kirk with the Church of England, forced him to call parliament to raise money. Exasperated by his illegal imposts, the Commons demanded redress of grievances first.

Anne of Denmark

Charles's attempt to arrest five leading members resulted in his flight from London, which he never succeeded in regaining. This put him at a hopeless disadvantage throughout the conflict with parliament; he was executed for treason seven years later.

Divine right

In the contest between Crown and parliament, both sides had genuine grievances. A poor communicator, Charles was so confident of his 'divine right' to rule that he was not prepared to persuade, conciliate or compromise, and regarded all opposition as, by definition, treasonous. The Commons, understanding little of the problems of government, were equally unreasonable.

'Royal martyr'

The execution of the king shocked Europe, as well as most of his subjects. His dignity and courage restored royal prestige and inflicted a propaganda defeat on his opponents. Though he had been dishonest and unreliable, sacrificing loyal ministers to preserve his own position, he is still remembered as the royal martyr.

♛ Charles's patronage of the arts and appreciation of painting accounts for the large number of portraits of him.

♛ Charles, married to a Roman Catholic and sympathetic to the Arminian, high-church movement represented by Archbishop William Laud, was suspected of Roman Catholic sympathies.

♛ Charles wore two shirts to his execution because it was a cold day and he was afraid that if he shivered people would think he was afraid.

Charles I

The English Civil Wars

King Charles I, who came to the throne in 1625, was stubborn, high-principled and convinced of his divine right to rule. Parliament regarded Charles as a tyrant and insisted on its right to a share in government. Both were convinced of the justice of their cause and neither would back down. The inevitable result was civil war.

Following a Scottish invasion (1638), an Irish rebellion in Ulster (1641) and the break between king and parliament, war began in 1642. Parliament's control of London gave it a significant advantage. The royalists, with headquarters at Oxford, held most of the north and west. Early fighting favoured the royalists ('Cavaliers'), but Scottish aid and

Oliver Cromwell

the new troops of **Oliver Cromwell** (1599-1658) secured the victory of Marston Moor (1644) for parliament ('Roundheads'). The Battle of Naseby (1645) was decisive. The royal forces disintegrated and Charles surrendered to the Scots, who handed him over to the army of Cromwell and Sir Thomas Fairfax (1647). His intrigues with all parties made agreement impossible and provoked a second civil war, with the Scots now on Charles's side. Cromwell's New Model Army defeated them at Preston (1648). The trial and execution of the king, a 'cruel necessity' according to Cromwell, followed.

In 1649-51 Cromwell crushed support for Charles II in Scotland and Ireland. At Drogheda and Wexford his troops took brutal revenge for massacres of Ulster Protestants by Irish Catholics in 1641. The army was now the real power in the land. Parliamentary government during the Interregnum (1649-60) proved no less arbitrary than the king's. Various expedients were tried before Cromwell, the outstanding statesman of his time, was made Lord Protector (1653), with the authority of a king. His son Richard succeeded him (1658) but lacked his authority. Charles II was invited to reassume the Crown in 1660.

Battle of Marston Moor

Charles II

must know	did you know?
Born: St James's Palace, 29 May 1630 **Parents:** Charles I and Henrietta Maria **Ascended the throne:** 30 January 1649 (by right); restored 29 May 1660 **Coronation:** As King of Scots, Scone, 1 January 1651; as King of England, Westminster Abbey, 23 April 1661 **Authority:** King of Great Britain and Ireland **Married:** Catherine of Braganza, daughter of the King of Portugal **Children:** Three children still-born; about 17 illegitimate children, including the Duke of Monmouth (1649-85) **Died:** Whitehall, 6 February 1685 **Buried:** Westminster Abbey	With the death of Oliver Cromwell, it became clear that it was necessary to return a monarch to the throne. Following the restoration of the monarchy, Charles II rode into London on 26 May 1660. Parliament had, however, taken precautions to ensure that the king would be unable to become a tyrant. The king was no longer accorded absolute power and, in particular, parliament had control of the country's finances.

After Cromwell's victory at Worcester (1651) Charles fled first to France and later to the Netherlands. He was recalled to the throne by parliament in 1660 at the instigation of General Monck, with powers scarcely less than those of his father and a determination not to 'go on his travels again'. He presided over an extravagant court, and supported revival of the theatre (banned during the Commonwealth) and the founding of the Royal Society (1660).His reign was marked by disasters such as the Great Plague (1665) and the Fire of London (1666), in which Charles helped fight the flames. In renewed conflict with the Dutch, part of the British fleet was destroyed when the Dutch sailed unchallenged up the Medway (1672).

The 'Merry Monarch'

The king's return signalled a predictable upsurge of gaiety and permisiveness. The theatres, closed as houses of the devil by the Puritans, were reopened and staged a series of plays full of sexual innuendo, immoral situations and bawdy jokes. Charles himself openly consorted with a series of new mistresses, the most famous being the former orange-seller and actress Nell Gwynne.

Behind the scenes, though, Charles reinforced his position as king by detaching himself from the most frustrating power that parliament possessed: the right to grant him money.

Money problems

Royal revenue continued to be insufficient, largely due to profligate spending. Charles circumvented the problem by deceiving his ministers and accepting secret subsidies from France, cynically promising to reintroduce Roman Catholicism (though he did die a Roman Catholic himself).

An extended family

Charles had numerous mistresses, including the orange-seller Nell Gwynne, and bastards, several of them the ancestors of current dukes. One son, the Duke of Monmouth, became a rival to his Roman Catholic uncle, the future James II, and he attempted to seize the throne after Charles's death.

👑 The English coronation regalia had been broken up during the Interregnum. A new set had to be made in 1660.

👑 Charles and his brother James narrowly escaped assassination on their way from Newmarket races in the Rye House Plot (1683).

👑 The wittiest of British monarchs, Charles on his deathbed apologized to hovering courtiers for taking so long to die.

Charles I, the 'Merry Monarch'

James II

must know

Born: St James's Palace, 14 October 1633
Parents: Charles I and Henrietta Maria
Ascended the throne: 6 February 1685
Coronation: Westminster Abbey, 23 April 1685
Authority: King of Great Britain and Ireland
Married: (1) Anne Hyde, daughter of Edward Hyde, Earl of Clarendon, (2) Mary, daughter of the Duke of Modena
Children: With (1), four sons and four daughters, including the future sovereigns Mary II and Anne; with (2), two sons, including James Edward the 'Old Pretender', five daughters and five still-born babies
Deposed: 23 December 1688
Died: Château de Saint Germain-en-Laye, near Paris, 6 September 1701
Buried: Saint Germain-en-Laye; later, the church of the English Benedictines in Paris; possibly returned to Saint Germain

James had a good record as a soldier, naval commander and public servant. As an admitted Roman Catholic he was compelled to relinquish his offices by the Test Act (1673), but was gradually rehabilitated by Charles II, who resisted all attempts to promote a Protestant heir in James's place. The Duke of Monmouth, his nephew and Protestant rival to the throne, was defeated, but James's efforts to restore Roman Catholicism in England by packing parliament and dismissing opponents (including 75 per cent of JPs) aroused widespread antagonism, leading to his downfall.

The birth of a male heir (James Edward), implying a Roman Catholic succession, clinched James's fate. The rumour that the baby had been smuggled into the Queen's bed in a warming pan was wishful thinking. The birth prompted an invitation to William of Orange, married to James's Protestant daughter Mary, to take the Crown. James fled to France at Christmas 1688, having already sent Queen Mary and the infant James Edward to safety. In 1690 he attempted a comeback but was thwarted at the Battle of the Boyne in Ireland on 1 July. James returned to France as an exile and lived on until 1701. Towards the end it was said he suffered from some form of senility.

The king's wives

James married twice – on both occasions before he became king. His first wife was Anne Hyde, daughter of Edward Hyde, Earl of Clarendon and Lord Chancellor. She died young, aged 34, in 1671. This was a great misfortune for her husband and, in the long run, also for England as James' second wife, the Catholic Mary of Modena, innocently caused him to lose his throne.

Mary, who originally wanted to become a nun, was only 15 when she and James, 40, were married in 1673. After 15 years of marriage, and several miscarriages and still-births, she at last gave birth to a son who survived. However their joy was short-lived. The birth of their son was greeted with horror by the Anglicans: they now feared an endless line of Catholic monarchs on the throne of England. James was deposed soon after and the family fled to France.

A stiff-necked monarch

James did not plan to make himself a continental-style despot, nor to destroy the Church of England. He merely to sought to restore equality for Catholics. But his mulish temperament, narrow vision and willingness to ride roughshod over opponents made people think the worst.

♕ After their defeat at the Battle of Sedgemoor (1685), supporters of Monmouth's Rebellion in the West Country (1685) were brutally dealt with by Judge Jeffreys in the 'Bloody Assizes'.

♕ A trade boom that boosted royal revenue reduced James's dependence on parliament.

♕ Fleeing London in December 1688, James dropped the Great Seal of England in the River Thames.

James II

Mary II

must know

Born: St James's Palace, 30 April 1662
Parents: James II and Anne Hyde
Ascended the throne: 13 February 1689
Coronation: Westminster Abbey, 11 April 1689
Authority: Queen of England, Scotland and Ireland
Married: William of Orange
Children: None born alive
Died: Kensington Palace, 28 December 1694
Buried: Westminster Abbey

Mary had a cathartic effect on her husband William, who was renowned for his ill-temper. Viewed as a foreigner, the Dutch king's acceptance by his subjects depended on the queen. When she died, he withdrew himself, becoming even less popular. He had been devoted to Mary – when she died, William said 'You can imagine the state I am in, loving her as I do.'

The Glorious Revolution of 1688, also known as the Bloodless Revolution, arose out of the dire necessity to replace the Catholic King James II. The unexpected birth of a son by his second wife, Mary of Modena, opened up the prospect of a long line of Catholic monarchs. The throne was offered instead to James's Protestant daughter, Mary, and her husband, William of Orange, known as the Protestant Saviour of Europe.

Mary married her Dutch cousin at St James's Palace in 1677 when she was aged only 15. Despite her violent protestations at the time, their physical disparity (William was small, Mary large), lack of children, and William's preference for male company, it was a very successful match and Mary came to love her oftern boorish husband 'with a passion,' she said 'that cannot but end with my life' . Mary supported her husband's insistence that he should be king rather than merely consort. She was entirely subservient to him in affairs of state, but deputized adequately when he was absent abroad. Unlike her sister Anne, Mary showed little sympathy for her father, whose throne she had usurped, partly because of their religious differences. Mary inclined to the Calvinism of Holland, and the court observed a stricter code of morals than had been customary since 1660.

Smartening up the palace

William and Mary did not like living in Whitehall, which was drafty and bad for the king's asthma. They preferred Hampton Court and, especially, Kensington Palace, both greatly expanded by Sir Christopher Wren.

Royal sisters

William was responsible for reconciling Mary with her younger sister, Anne, with whom she was on bad terms for several years. He also pleased Anne when he appointed John Churchill, later Duke of Marlborough, and the husband of Anne's close friend, commander-in-chief, in spite of his involvement in intrigues against the throne. When Mary died, William reigned alone with Anne's approval.

♛ When Mary arrived in England to be proclaimed queen, it was reported by Sarah Churchill, who disliked both William and Mary, that she looked 'into every closet and conveniency, and turning up the quilts upon the bed, as people do when they come to an inn'. In reality, she had been warned that she must be cheerful and confident when she arrived in England, and in her enthusiasm, rather overdid it.

♛ Mary died of smallpox. William was with her when she died and was so devastated by grief that it was feared he might die too or lose his sanity. Though urged to marry again after Mary's death, William never did.

Mary II reigned with the Dutch William of Orange

William III

Born: The Hague, 4 November 1650
Parents: Prince William II of Orange, Stadtholder of the Netherlands, and Mary Henrietta, daughter of Charles I
Ascended the throne: 13 February 1689
Coronation: Westminster Abbey, 11 April 1689
Authority: King of England, Scotland and Ireland, Stadtholder of the Netherlands
Married: Mary, daughter of James II
Children: None born alive
Died: Kensington Palace, 8 March 1702
Buried: Westminster Abbey

William was already Stadtholder, virtually a hereditary monarch, of the Netherlands. The throne was offered to him and Mary jointly, a unique arrangement, as Mary was the actual heir but William insisted on being king. He reigned alone after Mary's death. There was practically no resistance to William in England when he landed at Brixham, but the deposed James II invaded Ireland in 1689, provoking a bloody campaign that terminated in William's victory at the Battle of the Boyne in 1690. Supporters of James in Scotland were defeated at Killiecrankie and Dunkeld. William was a Dutch patriot with wide political horizons: his first commitment was to a European alliance against French aggrandizement. France became, and long remained, Britain's enemy too.

The Bill of Rights

When William deposed James, clearing the way to the throne for his wife, he refused to become regent for the exiled King James. The deal was King William or no William and he threatened to return to Holland. Parliament capitulated and, in an arrangement unique in the history of the English monarchy, made them joint monarchs. However, parliament made William and Mary sign the Bill of Rights, the constitutional settlement of 1689. This would curtail royal power over important questions such as raising an army and freedom of speech within the House of Commons.

A Protestant champion

Now positioned as an equal, as a monarch, William sought to end his struggle with Louis XIV of France by utilising England's resources. William's lifelong resistance to the mighty Louis XIV of France made him the Protestant champion of Europe. Though physically small and not strong, he proved himself a good soldier as well as a diplomat. He was never, however, very popular in England.

♕ William died a few days after a fall when his horse stumbled over a molehill. Jacobites used to toast the 'little gentleman in black velvet' responsible for the accident.

♕ Archbishop Sancroft declined to crown William III, having crowned James II four years earlier, so the Bishop of London performed the ceremony.

William III

Anne

Born: St James's Palace, 6 February 1665
Parents: James II and Anne Hyde
Ascended the throne: 8 March 1702
Coronation: Westminster Abbey, 23 April 1702
Authority: Queen of Great Britain and Ireland
Married: George, son of Frederick III of Denmark
Children: 18, including those still-born and miscarried
Died: Kensington Palace, 1 August 1714
Buried: Westminster Abbey

The Peace of Utrecht was signed during the reign of Queen Anne. The terms of the agreement led to the establishment of new boundaries within Europe, with the redistribution of land and power. Although the War of the Spanish Succession had been fought over 11 long years, the signing of such a 'give-and-take' agreement was a turning point in the way grievances were solved.

Anne was an amiable and dutiful woman who presided over government without getting too involved in the intricacies of administration or the arguments of Whigs and Tories, though she favoured the latter and was devoted to the Anglican Church. She was not particularly intelligent, and her husband was notoriously dim, though amiable. Their sorrow was that, in spite of 18 pregnancies, none of Anne's children survived infancy except for one boy, who reached 11. Anne was given to intense female friendships, first with the Duchess of Marlborough, whose husband's victories over the French lent the Crown reflected glory, and later with Abigail Masham.

Prince George of Denmark

The United Kingdom

The Act of Union between England and Scotland (1707) made Anne the first sovereign of the United Kingdom. Though the Scots lost their parliament, they retained their own religious and legal systems. Union also reduced the danger of the Scots opting for a Jacobite succession.

A square coffin

Anne's health was poor. She suffered from gout and was unable to walk up the aisle at her coronation. Her ill luck as a mother may have caused her to overeat – and drink. Like her sister Mary, she was large, and grew larger. Her coffin was said to be almost cubic in shape.

♛ Like her ancestor, Henry VIII, Anne was sometimes moved about with the aid of chairs and pulleys.

♛ The Duke of Marlborough was dismissed in 1711 by a Tory ministry resentful of the cost of the British involvement in the War of the Spanish Succession (1702-13).

♛ A Jacobite 'pretender', backed by France, made a sortie to Scotland in 1708, but was prevented from landing.

Queen Anne

4 Hanover and Windsor

Charting an unsettled period of history that saw executive power gradually move from the monarch to the prime minister and cabinet, this section looks at the royal timeline from George I to Elizabeth II. These 300 or so years of history include Queen Victoria's 64 year reign – the longest of any British monarch – and the shock abdication of Edward VIII.

The Hanoverians

When it became clear that Queen Anne, like her sister, would not provide an heir, the Act of Settlement was passed in 1701 to prevent a Jacobite restoration. It settled the succession on the elderly Electress Sophia of Hanover, who was the granddaughter of James I through her mother, Elizabeth, wife of Frederick V, King of Bohemia (the 'Winter King'). She was, of course, a Protestant. As Sophia died two months before Anne, the Crown was inherited by her son George, Elector of Hanover since the death of his father in 1698.

Lack of familiarity with British affairs on the part of the first two Hanoverian kings assisted the gradual transfer of executive power from the monarch to the prime minister and cabinet.

Despite continuing threats from Jacobite claimants, the Hanoverian line continued uninterrupted through five monarchs. In 1837 the Crown descended to Queen Victoria, six generations removed from George I, while Hanover, where female succession was forbidden, passed to a male descendant of George III. Victoria married Prince Albert of Saxe-Coburg-Gotha, whose family name was **Wettin**, in 1840. In 1917, when Britain was at war with Germany, George V adopted the name **Windsor** for his dynasty. Elizabeth II, though married to a Mountbatten (itself an Anglicization of the German 'Battenberg') perpetuated the name Windsor by proclamation but revised her decision in 1960 so that the third generation of her male descendants should bear the name **Mountbatten-Windsor**.

George I

George I

must know

Born: Osnabrück, Hanover, 28 May 1660
Parents: Ernest Augustus, Elector of Hanover, and Sophia, daughter of Elizabeth of Bohemia
Ascended the throne: 1 August 1714
Coronation: Westminster Abbey, 20 October 1714
Authority: King of Great Britain and Ireland, Elector of Hanover
Married: Sophia Dorothea of Celle
Children: One son, the future George II, and one daughter; three illegitimate children
Died: Osnabrück, 11 June 1727
Buried: Leineschlosskirche, Hanover; reinterred Herrenhausen, Hanover, 1957

did you know?

George I left his wife behind when he moved from Hanover to England. Having divorced her and had her imprisoned for adultery, he arrived in England with two mistresses. George was generally regarded with suspicion and was disliked by his new subjects. He had failed to realise that he had to earn the respect and trust of his new subjects, and that they expected him to behave with grace and dignity.

George ascended the English throne with only a slight knowledge of English. He communicated with his ministers in French. He left his wife, from whom he was divorced, behind but brought to England two German mistresses, one skinny, one fat, and both incredibly ugly. The two ladies were promptly nicknamed, for obvious reasons, 'the Maypole' and 'the Elephant'. The first mistress, perhaps his wife (a secret marriage was rumoured), he made Duchess of Kendal. The other was also his half-sister and was made Countess of Darlington.

George preferred Hanover to his new kingdom and returned frequently. He never established much empathy with his British subjects. He was a gift to the gossips and humourists of the day: he was a dull man with florid features and bulging eyes. He reputedly had only three main interests in life: women, horses and food.

Britain's first prime minister

George was inevitably dependent on his ministers, especially Robert Walpole, the Whig magnate and political leader often called the first prime minister – the title did not become official until 1905– though the term was originally used mockingly. Walpole gained power through his skilful handling of the disastrous stock-market crash known as the South Sea Bubble (1720) and held it for over 20 years.

Family problems

George was a stolid, unimaginative man, despite his patronage of Handel, and out of his depth as a king in an alien country. His reputation was nevertheless somewhat sinister. He kept his wife a prisoner, with no access to her children, and was widely suspected of responsibility for the mysterious disappearance of her lover, Count Königsmarck, in 1694. Like his descendants, George I also quarrelled with his son and heir.

♔ George was anxious to keep abreast with the vogue for agricultural improvement. He once suggested planting turnips in St James's Park.
♔ George died of a stroke at Osnabrück after overeating on his way to Hanover.

George II

must know

Born: Herrenhausen, Hanover, 30 October 1683
Parents: George I and Sophia Dorothea of Celle
Ascended the throne: 11 June 1727
Coronation: Westminster Abbey, 11 October 1727
Authority: King of Great Britain and Ireland
Married: Caroline, daughter of the Margrave of Brandenburg-Ansbach
Children: Four sons and five daughters; probably one or more illegitimate children
Died: Kensington Palace, 25 October 1760
Buried: Westminster Abbey

George II spoke fluent English but with a strong accent, and he remained more German than English. He inherited a politically stable, economically prosperous and expanding kingdom, and a powerful minister, Walpole, whose survival, in spite of George's initial dislike, was largely due to his close working relationship with the intelligent and worldly Queen Caroline (died 1737). Constitutional monarchy was becoming firmly established. Like his father, whom he detested, George hated his own eldest son, Frederick, Prince of Wales (1707-51), who died, to his father's ill-disguised glee, after being struck by a cricket ball.

Foundations of empire

The contest with France for world-wide commercial supremacy and the foundations of the British Empire were taking shape in George's reign, culminating in the military and naval victories of the Seven Years' War (1756-63). British success was founded on the profits of agriculture and trade, which created investment capital and increasing industrial production.

'Devil take the whole island'

George resembled his father in appearance, in his liking for Handel – he originated the custom of standing up for the 'Hallelujah Chorus' in the *Messiah* – and in his preference for Hanover to England which, in a temper, he once consigned to the devil.

👑 One visible sign of economic growth was the building of turnpikes, the first national road system since the Romans.

👑 Dick Turpin, the famous highwayman, was arrested and executed in 1739.

👑 George II was the last British monarch to lead his troops on the battlefield, against the French at Dettingen in 1743 in the War of the Austrian Succession, and the last to be buried at Westminster.

👑 Government measures to reduce the appalling consumption of gin provoked a mob to harass the royal coach, shouting, 'No Gin, No King!'

Queen Caroline II

George III

must know

Born: Norfolk House, St James's Square, London, 4 June 1738
Parents: Frederick, Prince of Wales, and Augusta, daughter of the Duke of Saxe-Coburg-Gotha
Ascended the throne: 25 October 1760
Coronation: Westminster Abbey, 22 September 1761
Authority: King of the United Kingdom of Great Britain and Ireland, Elector (later King) of Hanover
Married: Charlotte, daughter of the Duke of Mecklenburg-Strelitz
Children: Ten sons, including the future George IV and William IV, and six daughters
Died: Windsor, 29 January 1820
Buried: St George's Chapel, Windsor

did you know?

The so-called 'madness' of King George is thought to have been caused by porphyria, a genetic disorder that disturbs the normal metabolism of the body and produces the symptoms that in the eighteenth century appeared to be insanity. Medical science knew little about mental illness at this time, and barbaric, completely ineffective treatments served to deteriorate, rather then help, the king's condition.

George III inherited the throne on a tide of domestic prosperity and martial victory. He prided himself on being British to the core and, with his amiable queen, echoed the tastes and prejudices of the rising middle class. Anxious to restore royal powers that had dwindled under his predecessors, he was practically the last monarch able to a large extent to choose his own ministers, and ended half a century of Whig dominance. His reign was clouded by periodic attacks of insanity, now known to have been symptoms of porphyria. His last attack (1810) proved permanent and his heir was proclaimed Prince Regent in February 1811.

George III and Lord Howe

An imperial setback

Growing disagreements between the British government and the North American colonists led to the American Declaration of Independence (1776) and successful rebellion. The king was widely blamed for the loss of the 13 colonies and is still popularly regarded as a wicked despot in the United States.

'Farmer George'

Dutiful, hard-working and genial, in spite of the revolutionary times, George made the monarchy more popular. He delighted in his nickname, born of his experimental farms in Windsor Park.

Buckingham Palace

Buckingham Palace, in the Mall, is the official London residence of the reigning monarch. It has been at the focus of great national events such as royal weddings, births, coronations and the celebrations that took place at the end of the Second World War in 1945. It was officially built between 1702 and 1705 for John Sheffield, first Duke of Buckingham, and was, at that time, called Buckingham House. George purchased it in 1761 when it was still a country house on the rural outskirts of London.

👑 George survived at least one assassination attempt, displaying commendable coolness under fire.

👑 The French Revolution and ensuing wars with France led to fears of invasion before the combined French and Spanish fleets were destroyed by Nelson at Trafalgar (1805).

👑 George fiercely, and successfully, opposed measures to restore the civil rights of Roman Catholics.

George III

weblink: http://www.royal.gov.uk/output/Page111.asp

George IV

Born: St James's Palace, 12 August 1762
Parents: George III and Charlotte of Mecklenburg-Strelitz
Ascended the throne: 29 January 1820
Coronation: Westminster Abbey, 19 July 1821
Authority: King of the United Kingdom of Great Britain and Ireland, King of Hanover
Married: Caroline, daughter of the Duke of Brunswick
Children: One daughter, Charlotte Augusta; two illegitimate children
Died: Windsor, 26 June 1830
Buried: St George's Chapel, Windsor

According to Hanoverian custom, the Prince of Wales was on poor terms with his father, whom he effectively succeeded when he became Prince Regent in 1811. An amiable, self-indulgent dandy with romantic illusions about himself (in old age he insisted he had fought at the Battle of Waterloo), he was the darling of society until he grew fat and over-extravagant. He married Caroline in 1795 only because parliament promised to pay his debts. Dislike was mutual, and though a bill to dissolve the marriage was dropped, Caroline was forcibly barred from the coronation. George was the first Hanoverian monarch to visit Ireland and Scotland (1822), wearing Highland dress – Stuart tartan – with some élan and winning over many with his charm.

The coronation of George IV

Wives and mistresses

The worst Hanoverian vice seems to have been a passion for 'the ladies'. A seemingly endless stream of women surrounded George IV for most of his life. For the duration of these affairs he lavished money and affection upon the woman in question. His behaviour toward his wife, Caroline, however, showed a marked contrast.

O'Connell takes his seat

Elected MP for County Clare in 1828, Daniel O'Connell was debarred from parliament as a Roman Catholic. The Catholic Emancipation Act was forced through by the reforming home secretary, Sir Robert Peel, in 1829, with the backing of the Duke of Wellington but against the wishes of George IV.

Oriental fantasy

Although Parliament and others were appalled by the Prince Regent's extravagance, posterity has some reason to be grateful. Most notable of his artistic projects was the fairy-tale palace known as Brighton Pavilion.

♔ In 1785 George secretly, and illegally, married the most persistent of his many mistresses, Mrs Fitzherbert.
♔ When George first set eyes on the vulgar German princess he had agreed to marry, it is said he turned pale and asked for brandy.
♔ When the popular Princess Charlotte died in childbirth in 1817, George's brothers hastened to marry and produce heirs.

The extravagant George VI

William IV

must know

Born: Buckingham Palace, 21 August 1765
Parents: George III and Charlotte of Mecklenburg-Strelitz
Ascended the throne: 26 June 1830
Coronation: Westminster Abbey, 8 September 1831
Authority: King of the United Kingdom of Great Britain and Ireland, King of Hanover
Married: Adelaide, daughter of the Duke of Saxe-Meinigen
Children: Four, none of whom survived infancy
Died: Windsor, 20 June 1837
Buried: St George's Chapel, Windsor

did you know?

Known as 'Silly Billy', William IV made an unlikely king. He was a bluff, excitable, boorish man who wore his hair in a quiff and was little respected, with poor manners and morals. He was reputedly so pleased to become king that he rode around London in his carriage, grinning broadly at his new subjects, offering them lifts and even kissing some of them.

As Duke of Clarence and third son of George III, William IV had not expected to become king and always behaved more like a retired naval officer, which he was, than a monarch. He had a large family with an actress known as Mrs Jordan before marrying a young German princess in 1818. This attempt to produce an heir was unsuccessful, but Adelaide was a kindly stepmother to the brood of 'Fitzclarences'. Well-meaning but tactless, William lacked George IV's intelligence and charm but was more committed to duty and generally supported his ministers even when he disliked their policy.

Parliamentary reform

Parliament had degenerated since the days when it challenged the authority of kings and had pioneered its own supremacy in government with the establishment of the constitutional monarchy in 1689. The corruption which had fuelled its proceedings in the eighteenth century had combined with social changes to make parliament unrepresentative and full of inequalities. Not least of these was an imbalance between the representation of rural communities and the new industrial towns,

The answer and the political centrepiece of William's reign was the Great Reform Act (1832), the first step on the road to universal franchise. William agreed to the request of Lord Grey, the prime minister, to dissolve the hostile parliament and put some pressure on the Lords to prevent the bill's defeat, though, worried by republicanism, he later got rid of Grey.

Crowned 'on the cheap'

The coronation of William and Adelaide was in marked contrast to the gorgeous affair designed for himself by George IV. William insisted on economies, the usual banquet was cancelled, and Adelaide provided the jewels for her crown.

👑 The number of pubs called 'Queen Adelaide' testifies to the popularity of William IV's sweet-natured queen.

👑 Six Dorset farm labourers, the 'Tolpuddle Martyrs', were transported to Australia in 1834 for conspiring to form a trade union.

👑 In 1836 the South African Boers set out on the 'Great Trek' to escape British control of Cape Colony.

William IV, an unpopular monarch

Victoria

must know

Born: Kensington Palace, 24 May 1819
Parents: Edward, Duke of Kent, and Victoria, daughter of the Duke of Saxe-Coburg-Saalfeld
Ascended the throne: 20 June 1837
Coronation: Westminster Abbey, 28 June 1838
Authority: Queen of the United Kingdom of Great Britain and Ireland, Empress of India (from 1 May 1876)
Married: Albert, son of the Duke of Saxe-Coburg-Gotha
Children: Four sons, including the future Edward VII, and five daughters
Died: Osborne, Isle of Wight, 22 January 1901
Buried: Frogmore, Windsor

During Victoria's reign, the longest of any British monarch, the Crown lost virtually all executive power but became a potent national symbol, representing constancy and stability in changing times. Victoria's sense of duty and her sympathy with the opinions of the dominant middle class were augmented by Albert, created Prince Consort in 1857, a man of ability and diligence. His early death in 1861 plunged her into prolonged and secluded mourning, causing her to temporarily lose some popularity.

Royal morals before Victoria had been so outrageous, culminating with the vulgar, quarrelsome Hanoverian kings, that a puritan-style reaction was bound to set in at some point. Albert was so puritan in his outlook that he confessed to feeling physically ill whenever he thought of marital infidelity. The impressionable Victoria, utterly devoted to Albert, adopted a similar attitude, despite there being reason to believe that she had inherited much of the passionate Hanoverian temperament.

Progress and order

In spite of the tensions caused by rapid social and economic change, for most of Victoria's reign Britain was extraordinarily orderly. Political violence was rare after 1848 when the Chartists, demanding political reforms, staged a protest in London. Crime actually decreased. Education and democracy made large advances, while social reforms ameliorated the hardships of industrialization.

The Diamond Jubilee

This event on 22 June 1897 was not simply a thanksgiving for a long and largely peaceful reign – it was a dazzling celebration of the Empire. Victoria, Empress of India since 1876, reigned over a larger expanse of territory than any British monarch before her, covering one quarter of the Earth's land surface. The Diamond Jubilee was therefore an occasion to advertise Britain's greatness.

The royal 'we'

Queen Victoria has been mocked for saying 'we' when referring to herself. It resulted from her reluctance to dissociate Prince Albert, even after his death, from her own views. In later life she denied making the famous remark, 'We are not amused.'

♕ Victoria could not conceal her preferences among her ministers, adoring the Conservative Benjamin Disraeli (prime minister 1868, 1874-80), and loathing the Liberal William Gladstone (prime minister 1868-74, 1880-5, 1886, 1892-4).
♕ At Victoria's accession, the fastest transport was the horse. By her death, trains were being challenged by motor cars.
♕ At Victoria's death, few of her subjects were old enough to remember life under another monarch.

Queen Victoria reigned for 64 years

Edward VII

must know

Born: Buckingham Palace, 9 November 1841
Parents: Victoria and Albert
Ascended the throne: 22 January 1901
Coronation: Westminster Abbey, 9 August 1902
Authority: King of Great Britain and Ireland and of British Dominions overseas, Emperor of India
Married: Alexandra, daughter of Christian IX of Denmark
Children: Three sons, including the future George V, and three daughters
Died: Buckingham Palace, 6 May 1910
Buried: St George's Chapel, Windsor

did you know?

Edward VII was an unruly youth, and did not live up to his parents' expectations. They intended to produce intellectually brilliant, morally upright, impeccably respectable children. Edward preferred to socialize with friends and visit the theatre and race track rather than pursue intellectual pastimes. When his father died, Victoria partly blamed Edward.

In character the pleasure-loving Edward VII was most unlike his parents. He enjoyed a social and sporting life, and, as Prince of Wales, was linked with several scandals which gave his mother an excuse for excluding him from royal duties other than purely ceremonial ones. He visited North America and India among other state visits, and his genial nature and love of ceremonial occasion made him widely popular. His personal influence helped to cement the Entente Cordiale between Britain and France, though he was less successful with his nephew, the German Emperor, whom he disliked.

Entente Cordiale

The Entente Cordiale of 1904 saw the coming together of two old enemies in mutual defence against the rising new power in Europe. France's border with Germany had been crossed by Prussian forces in 1870 and she had not forgotten the humiliation. The German naval armament programme and the militaristic nature of Kaiser Wilhelm II forced the British out of their 'magnificent isolation' from the continent.

Social welfare

Following the victory of the Liberals in the general election of 1906, the first steps were taken towards the creation of a welfare state with the introduction of national insurance and old-age pensions. The Liberal programme led to a constitutional crisis in 1910 when the Tory-dominated Lords refused to pass Liberal legislation.

Edward VII

No votes for women

Like most monarchs Edward was a conservative, to whom democracy was anathema. In the face of the growing suffragette movement, founded by Emmeline Pankhurst in 1903, he opposed granting women the vote. The vote for women – but at first only those over the age of 30 – did not come until 1918, after women had proved themselves in the First World War by taking over men's jobs during the hostilities.

♛ Edward VII was the only monarch of the dynasty of Saxe-Coburg-Gotha, or House of Wettin. The name was changed as it was considered too Germanic.

♛ Edward ate five large meals every day, dinner usually running to at least ten courses.

♛ Though his reign was short, Edward gave his name to an age which in many ways he personified.

George V

Born: Marlborough House, London, 3 June 1865
Parents: Edward VII and Alexandra
Ascended the throne: 6 May 1910
Coronation: Westminster Abbey, 22 June 1911
Authority: King of Great Britain and Ireland and British Dominions overseas, Emperor of India
Married: Mary, daughter of the Duke of Teck
Children: Five sons, including the future Edward VIII and George VI, and one daughter
Died: Sandringham, Norfolk, 20 January 1936
Buried: St George's Chapel, Windsor

Like William IV, George V was a younger son who was not expected to become king and therefore served in the navy. He retained a certain informality, which suited his simple, straightforward character and reinforced his popularity. He proved to be the model modern monarch by carrying out his royal responsibilities with exemplary dedication while maintaining an irreproachable personal and family life, although, like many predecessors, he fell out with the Prince of Wales. On several occasions he

George V with his family

showed that the monarch's right to advise could be significant, especially in pressing for an end to the violence in Ireland, 1919-21.

The First World War

A century of relative peace in Europe ended in 1914 with the outbreak of the First World War, in which nearly one million British subjects were killed and two-and-a-half million wounded. Among other casualties were several European monarchies, but in spite of tumultuous social and political changes the British monarchy emerged intact.

Changing the royal name

As the horrors of the First World War filtered into public knowledge in Britain there was an upsurge of popular rage against the Germans. This put the royal family in an awkward position. The wartime king, George, the second monarch of the House of Saxe-Coburg-Gotha, belonged to the seventh generation of the Hanoverian dynasty.

George therefore decided that , first of all, members of the royal family must give up their German titles, and secondly that the name of the family and the dynasty had to be changed. On 19 June 1917, it was announced that the new royal name was to be Windsor. Even so, the slur of German ancestry did not disappear: Edward VIII would later be suspected of pro-Nazi sympathies before and during the Second World War.

His favourite opera

Unlike his artistically inclined queen, George V cared nothing for the arts and admitted to uncultured tastes. He once said that his favourite opera was *La Bohème*, because it was 'the shortest'.

♛ George V's elder brother, Clarence, who died in 1892, had a doubtful reputation. George was a much steadier character.
♛ King George and Queen Mary were crowned emperor and empress of India in a fabulous ceremony at the Delhi Durbar on 12 December 1911.
♛ George V was the first monarch to make a Christmas Day broadcast to the nation.

Edward VIII

<table>
<tr><td>

must know

Born: White Lodge, Richmond, Surrey, 23 June 1894
Parents: George V and Mary of Teck
Ascended the throne: 20 January 1936
Coronation: Never crowned
Authority: King of Great Britain and Ireland and British Dominions overseas, Emperor of India
Married: Mrs Wallis Simpson
Children: None
Died: Paris, 28 May 1972
Buried: Frogmore, Windsor

</td><td>

did you know?

Edward VIII had a strict and largely loveless upbringing where duty was all. His parents, King George V and Queen Mary, had very different ideas on kingship. George V believed that a monarch should be aloof and preserve royal dignity with distance, while Edward had an unconventional and more personal approach which was unacceptable to them.

</td></tr>
</table>

George V's eldest son, known as David to the royal family, appeared an ideal Prince of Wales. However, no prince or king in recent British history had broken the rules of monarchy to the extent that Edward did. Handsome and charming, a great success on public occasions and foreign visits, he also expressed sympathy with the unemployed. His predeliction for fashionable society and for older, married women worried his father, and he resented George V's refusal to allow him to serve at the front during the first world war. He insisted on going to the trenches in France to meet and talk with British soldiers. He sat with them amid the mud and slime in which they lived and fought. The soldiers loved him for it, but many people considered such behaviour inappropriate for a royal. Edward, however, refused to be distant and his behaviour became increasingly unprincely. The culmination of his abandonment of the royal code led to his abdication. On succeeding to the throne, his plan to marry Mrs Wallis Simpson, an American divorcée, provoked a constitutional crisis ending in his abdication after 11 months. Created Duke of Windsor (1937), he lived the rest of his life abroad.

The prince and the Nazis

Edward's political naïvety led him to make unwisely approving remarks about the Nazi regime in Germany during the 1930s. In 1937, as Duke of Windsor, Edward and his duchess accepted an invitation to visit Nazi Germany and were treated with great deference and maximum publicity by the Nazi Führer, Adolf Hitler.

With war against Germany fast looming at the time, the visit gave rise to talk that the duke was a Nazi sympathiser.

Suggestions that he was a traitor to Britain during the Second World War, during which he served as Governor of the Bahamas (1940-45), and that he hoped to regain the throne after a German invasion, seem to be exaggerated.

Wallis under wraps

The British press agreed to conceal the king's liaison with Mrs Simpson. Pictures showing them together were censored, but as they appeared in foreign papers, the affair gradually became public knowledge.

👑 Edward VIII's moving broadcast on his abdication on 11 December 1936 was partly drafted by Winston Churchill, a supporter.

👑 Influenced by his wife and his affinity with the United States, the Duke of Windsor spoke with a slight American accent.

👑 Ten days before his death, the Duke was visited at his home by his niece, Elizabeth II, in a symbolic gesture of reconciliation.

Edward VIII

weblink: http://news.bbc.co.uk/1/hi/uk/2701463.stm

George VI

must know

Born: Sandringham, Norfolk, 14 December 1895
Parents: George V and Mary of Teck
Ascended the throne: 11 December 1936
Coronation: Westminster Abbey, 12 May 1937
Authority: King of the United Kingdom of Great Britain and Northern Ireland and
British Dominions overseas, Emperor of India (until 1947)
Married: Elizabeth Bowes-Lyon, daughter of the Earl of Strathmore
and Kinghorne
Children: Two daughters, the future Elizabeth II and Margaret
Died: Sandringham, 6 February 1952
Buried: St George's Chapel, Windsor

In the tradition of younger sons, Prince Albert ('Bertie': he adopted the name
George in tribute to his father) served in the navy and was later created Duke of York.
Shy, with a stammer that made public speaking an ordeal, he was appalled to be
summoned to the throne at three weeks' notice after Edward VIII's abdication,
and so was his wife.

With all his father's transparent decency and devotion to duty, and an underlying
humility (despite occasional flashes of Hanoverian temper), he proved an ideal
figurehead during the Second World War.

In the months leading up to the outbreak of war, the king supported the policy of
appeasement that his prime minister, Neville Chamberlain, had adopted. The last thing
George wanted was to involve his country in another war on the scale of that which
had raged between 1914 1nd 1918 at the cost of nearly one million lives. By summer
1939, however, it became clear to Chamberlain that negotiations were not going to
work, and at 11 a.m. on 3 September 1939, Chamberlain broadcasted to the nation:
'This country is now at war with Germany'.

The king kept a very public profile for the duration of the war. He visited factories,
hospitals and military bases. Refusing to leave London, the king and queen did
wonders for Londoners' morale during the Blitz, narrowly escaping death themselves
when Buckingham Palace was hit.

The Second World War

Britain was at war for nearly half of George VI's reign, and in 1940-41, in spite of support from the empire, especially the Dominions, it appeared to be in danger of defeat. The great changes that war brought, or expedited, included the relinquishing of empire. George VI lost his imperial title with Indian independence in 1947 and became head of the (British) Commonwealth in 1949.

Indian independence

When India gained its independence on 15 August 1947, it was one of the most momentous events of the twentieth century. This was not simply because two new nations – India and Pakistan – came into being, but because it signalled the end of an era: the era of European empires overseas, of which the British empire had been the largest. Of all the far-flung territories of this empire, India, the first to become indendent, had been regarded as the 'jewel in the crown'.

Doubts about prime ministers

When Neville Chamberlain resigned as prime minister in May 1940, the king would have preferred Lord Halifax to Churchill, who had a reputation as a political maverick. However, their relationship ripened into mutual admiration and friendship. In 1945 he was similarly cool, at first, towards the Labour prime minister, Clement Attlee.

♛ George VI restored the popularity of the monarchy, damaged by the Abdication Crisis.
♛ In the 1930s the king's stammer was much reduced, though not quite cured, by an Australian speech therapist.
♛ From childhood George VI suffered frequent illness. He died not long after an operation for lung cancer.

George VI

Elizabeth II

must know

Born: 17 Bruton Street, London, 21 April 1926
Parents: George VI and Elizabeth Bowes-Lyon
Ascended the throne: 6 February 1952
Coronation: Westminster Abbey, 2 June 1953
Authority: Queen of the United Kingdom of Great Britain and Northern Ireland,
Head of the Commonwealth
Married: Philip, son of Prince Andrew of Greece
Children: Three sons, Charles, Andrew and Edward, and one daughter, Anne

The Queen inherited her father's devotion to duty, simple tastes and fondness for family life. She became officially engaged to Prince Philip, an officer in the Royal Navy, in 1947, and he was created Duke of Edinburgh. He brought vigour and informality to the royal family, at the cost of occasional breaches of tact. The Queen was criticized for being out of touch during an anti-monarchical period around 1957, but has otherwise commanded widespread respect and affection. The prestige of royalty, however, was seriously damaged by the much publicized failures of the marriages of, first, her sister, Princess Margaret, and later of three of her children, including the Prince of Wales.

The relationship between sovereigns of England and their subjects has changed a great deal over the centuries. Consequently, the public behaviour of kings and queens has varied from godlike and aloof to the dignified but friendly approach of royals today. It was Elizabeth's parents who broke new ground during the Second World War. At this time they personally toured areas of London destroyed during the Blitz and chatted with families, the victims of the bombing. Even so, the separation between royal and commoner, sovereign and subject, was still evident.

The Commonwealth

During the reign of Elizabeth II, Britain has relinquished the last remnants of empire apart from a few minor territories. A shadow of empire remained in the Commonwealth, an association of Anglophone nations, some of which acknowledged the Queen as ceremonial head of state, but the Suez affair (1956) demonstrated Britain's international weakness.

The Suez Crisis

Egypt was never formally a colony of the British Empire, but the Suez Canal, an indispensable trade route to India and the Far East, had been occupied by Britain since 1936. In 1956 the Egyptian president, Gamal Abdel Nasser, announced the nationalization of the Suez Canal. This caused outrage and dismay in Britain in particular, which was a major shareholder in the canal.

Royal soap opera

Elizabeth II has played her dual role as representative of the people and symbol of the nation faultlessly, and has revealed more of her private life to the public than any predecessor. But the activities of some members of the royal family, publicized by ruthless news media, has threatened to turn the royal family into a source of cheap entertainment.

👑 Elizabeth II's reign has become the longest this century and one of the longest in British history.

👑 Elizabeth's crown, now in the Tower of London, was made in 1660 out of gold, with over 400 precious and semi-precious stones.

👑 To defuse criticism of royal wealth, the Queen agreed to pay taxes on her private income.

👑 Since there is no tradition of abdication, in the event of Elizabeth's incapacity the probable solution would be a regency.

👑 Elizabeth II has made more state visits than any previous monarch.

Elizabeth II

Illustration Notes

All pictures were supplied courtesy of the Bridgeman Art Library, London (coded BAL throughout), except for those individually credited below. Picture numbers precede the illustration reference.

10 Arms and Costume of a Saxon Military Chief (Private Collection). Courtesy of Hulton Deutsch Collection Limited, London. 11 Sestertius of Hadrian from Newcastle Upon Tyne. Shows Bust of Hadrian as a Victorious Commander (Museum of Antiquities, Newcastle Upon Tyne). BAL. 12 Arms and Costume of an Anglo-Saxon King and Armour-Bearer (Private Collection). Courtesy of Hulton Deutsch Collection Limited, London. 15 Macbeth Instructing the Murderers Employed to Kill Banquo, by George Cattermole (Victoria & Albert Museum, London). BAL. 16 17 King Malcolm III. Courtesy of Hulton Deutsch Collection Limited, London. 20 King Edgar Seated between Saint Dunstan and Saint Ethelwold, Christchurch, from Regularis Concorda and Rule of Saint Benedict (British Library, London). BAL. 21 King David I of Scotland. Courtesy of Hulton Deutsch Collection Limited. London. 22 David I, King of Scotland from 1124, and his successor, King Malcolm IV, King from 1153. Courtesy of Hulton Deutsch Collection Ltd. 23 William 'The Lion'. Courtesy of Hulton Deutsch Collection Ltd. 25 King Alexander III of Scotland. Courtesy of Hulton Deutsch Collection Limited, London. 26 Robert Bruce, from the Seton Armorial. Courtesy of The National Library of Scotland. 28 Bruce's Tomb, Dunfermline Abbey. Courtesy of The Still Moving Picture Company. 29 Bruce at Bannockburn. (Private Collection). 30 David II, King of Scotland from 1329. Courtesy of Hulton Deutsch Collection Limited, London. 31 Edward 'Lion', King of Scotland, Courtesy of Hulton Deutsch Collection Limited, London. 33 James I of Scotland, by Anonymous (Scottish National Portrait Gallery, Edinburgh). BAL. 34 James II of Scotland, by Anonymous (Scottish National Portrait Gallery, Edinburgh). BAL. 35 James III of Scotland by Anonymous (Scottish National Portrait Gallery, Edinburgh). 37 James IV of Scotland, by Anonymous (Scottish National Portrait Gallery, Edinburgh).BAL. 39 James V of Scotland, by Anonymous (Scottish National Portrait Gallery, Edinburgh). BAL. 40 Mary, Queen of Scots, by William 'Senior' Bone (Wallace Collection, London). BAL. 41 James VI of Scotland and I of England and Ireland, by Adam de Colone (Scottish National Portrait Gallery, Edinburgh). BAL. 42 The Execution of Mary, Queen of Scots, by Anonymous (Scottish National Portrait Gallery, Edinburgh). BAL. 44 King Cormac and Fair Eithne, by Thomas Wright. Courtesy of Hulton Deutsch Collection Limited, London. 45 Irish King, Brian Boru is killed by a Viking Soldier, in a Surprise Attack Whilst he is Praying in his Tent. Courtesy of Hulton Deutsch Collection Limited, London. 47 Richard II, Kings of England from 1377 to 1399, Knighting the Four Kings of Ireland (O'Neill, O'Connor, O'Brien and MacMorrogh), in Dublin. Courtesy of Hulton Deutsch Collection Limited, London. 55 Portrait of Owen Glyndwr, from his Great Seat, engraved from the Archæologia. Courtesy of The National Library of Wales. 56 Rhys Ap Gruffydd, The Lord Rhys. Courtesy of the National Library of Wales. 58 Llewelyn Ap Gruffydd. Courtesy of the National Library of Wales. 59 Owain Glyndwr. Courtesy of the National Library of Wales. 62 Treaty of Hengist and Horsa with Vortigern. Courtesy of Hulton Deutsch Collection. 63 The First Meeting of the British King Vortigern with the two Saxon Chiefs Hengist and Horsa. Courtesy of Hulton Deutsch Collection Limited, London. 64 Silver Penny of Ethelbert, Anglo-Saxon King of East Anglia (Private Collection). BAL. 66 Anglo Saxon Monarch, 8th Century. Courtesy of The Fotomas Index Picture Library, Kent. 68 Sigebert, the King-Monk, was Persuaded to Leave his Cell and Lead the Army Against Penda, King of Mercia, by S. Paget. Courtesy of Hulton Deutsch Collection Limited, London. 69 Detail of Illuminated Letter G: King Athelstan (British Library, London). BAL. 72 King Offa of Mercia Overseeing Builder Carrying Bricks (Trinity College, Dublin). BAL. 76 Egbert, King of the West Saxons. Courtesy of The Fotomas Index Picture Index Picture Library, Kent. 78 The Viking Sea Raiders, by Albert Goodwin (Christopher Wood Gallery, London). BAL. 80 Edward the Elder. Courtesy of The Fotomas Index Picture Library, Kent. 81 Malmesbury Abbey (Private Collection). 84 Detail from St Dunstan Crowning St. Edward the Martyr and his murder at Corfe Castle (Musée Conde, Chantilly). BAL. 84 Anglo Saxon Military Chief, Trumpeter and Warriors, etched by L. A. Arkinson. Courtesy of Hulton Deutsch Collection Limited, London. 86 The Danes Descend Upon the Coast and Possess Northumberland (Wallington Hall, Northumberland). BAL. 87 Vision of the Drowning of King Svein I Haraldsson Forkbeard of Denmark as He Embarked for England (Private Collection). BAL. 89 Cotton Manuscript: King Cnut, (British Library, London). BAL. 90 Harold I: Mary Evans Picture Library. 91 Edward the Confessor, by East Anglian School (Richard Philip, London). BAL. 92-93 The Death of Harold, from the Bayeux Tapestry (Topham Picturepoint). BAL. 95 The Death of King Edward, from the Bayeux Tapestry (Musée de la Tapisserie, Bayeux). BAL. 96 William the Conqueror receives Allegiance from his Nephew le Roux (British Library, London). BAL. 97 Portrait of William the Conqueror, by English School (Philip Mould, Historical Portraits Ltd, London). BAL. 99 William II, from Historia Anglorum (British Library, London). BAL. 101 Henry I Receiving News of the News of the Drowning of his Sons in the White Ship, by Anonymous (Hartlepool Museum Service, Hartlepool). BAL. 102 Silver Penny of Stephen (Private Collection). BAL. 103 King Stephen Enthroned, written during the reign of Edward II, from Chronicle of Peter of Langtoft (British Library, London). BAL. 105 Geoffrey Plantagenet (Private Collection). 106 The Murder of Becket. Courtesy of Scala. 107 Richard I from The Four Kings of England, from Historia Anglorum (British Library). BAL. 109 Henry II from The Four Kings of England, from Historia Anglorum (British Library). BAL. 111 King Richard I and His Barons, (British Library, London). BAL. 113 King John Hunting (British Library, London). BAL. 114 Parliament of The Period. (Private Collection). BAL. 115 Henry III Being Crowned (British Museum, London). BAL. 116 Edward I with Monks and Bishops, from the Cotton Manuscript (British Library, London). BAL. 117 The Siege of Berwick, by Edward I, 1297, English, with Flemish Illuminations, from Saint Albans's Chronicle, (Lambeth Palace Library, London). BAL. 118 Entry of Queen Isabella (British Library, London). BAL. 119 Marriage of Edward II to Isabella, daughter of Philip IV at Boulogne (British Library, London). BAL. 120 Edward III as founder of the Order of the Garter (British Library, London). BAL. 121 Edward III Granting the Black Prince the Principality of Aquitaine (Private Collection). BAL. 123 Richard II is taken into the Tower of London (British Library, London). BAL. 124 Henry Bolingbroke (Henry IV) enters London, executed for Edward IV (British Library, London). BAL. 125 Coronation of Henry IV, from Froissart's Chronicle (British Library, London). BAL. 126 Marriage of Henry V to Catharine of France, 1461 (British Library, London). BAL. 127 Morning of Agincourt, 25 October 1415, by Sir John Gilbert (Guildhall Art Gallery, Corporation of London). BAL. 128 The Crowning of Henry VI at Westminster, from English Psalter, 1470 (Victoria & Albert Museum, London). BAL. 129 Henry VI of England, by Francois Clouet (Manor House, Stanton Harcourt, Oxfordshire). BAL. 130 Edward IV in Council (British Library, London). BAL. 132 Edward IV of England Landing in Calais, from Memoirs of Philippe of Commines (Musée Thomas Dobree-Musée Archeologique, Nantes). Courtesy of Giraudon and The Bridgeman Art Library. 135 Richard III, by Anonymous (Syon House, Middlesex). BAL. 138 Elizabethan London Showing Shipping on the Thames, with Old London Bridge, engraving by Cornelius de Visscher (Guildhall Library, Corporation of London). BAL. 140 King Henry VII, by Anonymous (Royal Society of Arts, London). BAL. 141 Portrait of Henry VIII, by Hans Holbein (Belvoir Castle, Rutland). BAL. 144 Edward VI with the Chain of the Order of the Garter, by William Scrots (Richard Philp, London). BAL. 145 The Execution of Lady Jane Grey in the Tower of London in 1553, by Hippolyte Delaroche (National Gallery, London). BAL. 146-7 Queen Mary I, by William Scrots (Private Collection). BAL. 149 Elizabeth I, Armada Portrait, by Anonymous (Private Collection). BAL. 150 James I, Half-Length Portrait, by John the Elder Decritz (Roy Miles Gallery, London). BAL. 152 Anne of Denmark, by Marcus Gheeraerts (Woburn Abbey, Bedfordshire). BAL. 153 Charles I on Horseback, by Sir Anthony van Dyck (National Gallery, London). BAL. 154 Contemporary Portrait of Oliver Cromwell, by Anonymous (Private Collection). BAL. 155 Battle of Marston Moor, by John Barker (Cheltenham Art Gallery and Museums, Gloucestershire). BAL. 157 Charles II, by Wallerant Vaillant (Phillips, London). BAL. 159 Miniature of James II as the Duke of York, 1661, by Samuel Cooper (Victoria & Albert Museum, London). BAL. 161 Mary II, wife of William III, by William Wissing (Scottish National Portrait Gallery, Edinburgh). BAL. 163 King William III, by William Wissing (Holburne Museum, Bath). BAL. 164 Prince George of Denmark, married Queen Anne of England, 1683, by Michael Dahl (Institute of Directors, London). BAL. 165 Queen Anne, 1703, by Edmund Lilly (Blenheim Palace, Oxfordshire). 168 King George I, by Sir Godfrey Kneller (Institute of Directors, London). BAL. 170 King George II, 1759, by Robert Edge Pine (Audley End, Essex). BAL. 171 Caroline II, Queen of George II, by Charles Jervas (Guildhall Art Gallery, Corporation of London). BAL. 172 George III & Lord Howe, by Isaac Cruikshank (Guildhall Art Gallery, London). BAL. 173 Portrait of King George III, by Anonymous (Institute of Directors, London). BAL. 174 Westminster Abbey, Coronation of George IV, aqua-tint by F. C. Lewis (Guildhall Library, Corporation of London). BAL. 175 George IV in his Garter Robes, by Sir Thomas Lawrence (National Gallery of Ireland, Dublin). BAL. 177 King William IV, by Sir John Simpson (Crown Estate, Institute of Directors, London). BAL. 179 The Four Generations, Windsor Castle, 1899, Queen Victoria, by Sir William Quiller Orchardson (Russell-Cotes Art Gallery and Museum, Bournemouth). BAL. 181 Edward VII Receiving Maharajahs and Dignataries Prior to his Coronation, by A. E. Harris (Roy Miles Gallery, London). BAL. 182 Thanksgiving Service for George V and Queen Mary, 1935, byFrank Salisbury (Guildhall Art Gallery, London). BAL. 185 Prince of Wales, later King Edward VIII, by Sir William Orpen (Royal & Ancient Golf Club, Saint Andrew's). BAL. 187 King George VI, by Oswald Hornby Joseph Birley (Crown Estate/Institute of Directors, London). BAL. 189 Queen Elizabeth II, by Denis Fildes (Institute of Directors, London). BAL.